Multicultural Education:
From Theory to Practice

Multicultural Education: From Theory to Practice

Mal Leicester

NFER-NELSON

Published by The NFER-NELSON Publishing Company Ltd,
Darville House, 2 Oxford Road East,
Windsor, Berkshire SL4 1DF, England.

First Published 1989
© 1989 Mal Leicester

British Library Cataloguing in Publication Data
Leicester, Mal
  Multicultural education: from theory to practice.
  1. Great Britain. Multicultural education
  I. Title
  370.11'5

Photoset by David John Services Ltd, Slough
Printed in Great Britain by Billing & Sons Ltd, Worcester

ISBN   0 7005 1242X
Code   8314 02 1

Contents

List of Tables and Figures

Preface

All schools are aware of the idea of a multicultural approach to education. Some local education authorities are asking schools and colleges to produce their own anti-racist or multicultural policies. Even when such a request is not being made many teachers, in both multiracial and in predominantly white areas, are seeking to develop an education which is appropriate for culturally plural twentieth-century Britain.

Part I of this book provides a concise introduction to the background issues. A brief historical outline brings us to the present day; to the influential Swann Report of 1985 and the current 'Education Reform Act'. I have also attempted to give a clear and readable account of key theoretical issues and in Part II to move from theory to practice. Part III provides teachers and managers with specific suggestions and approaches and with actual examples of positive curriculum developments. Chapter 6 contains advice about professional development and the bibliography suggests further reading and offers information about various kinds of learning resources and curriculum support.

Curriculum development, though vital, is time and energy consuming and the development of multicultural education has been attended by controversies of various kinds. My intention has been to help teachers to develop their classroom practices with confidence; the confidence that comes from familiarity with the issues, understanding of theoretical aspects and ability to disentangle confusions and distinguish between positive and negative approaches. Therefore, in this book, theory and practice are linked and mutually supportive. I hope that parents, teachers, advisers and administrators who are concerned about good education for all children will find practical advice on translating ideals of multicultural education into classroom reality.

Acknowledgements

I am grateful to the Avon Education Authority for permission to draw on examples and documents relating to my previous work as their Adviser for Multicultural Education, and to the National Development Centre (Bristol University) and ALAOME (Association of LEA Advisory Officers for Multicultural Education) from whose documents I quote. I would also like to thank teachers at Avon's Multicultural Education Centre who developed some of the 'in service' initiatives described in Chapter 5 and, in particular, Mary Smith, for many of the ideas in Chapter 4. Finally, considerable gratitude to Sue Tall for her patient and perspicacious typing of the manuscript and to Barry Clarke for several helpful comments.

Part 1
THEORY

CHAPTER 1
Historical Perspective

The purpose of this first chapter is to provide a context for what follows subsequently on the theory and practice of multicultural education. Concise background information is offered about the development, in Britain, of anti-racist multicultural education. An historical perspective brings us to the Swann Report of 1985. An outline of that report is followed by further discussion of some of its major concerns about language, curriculum and race. Finally we come right up to the present day and the 'Great' Education Reform Act (ERA) (GB. DES, 1988). How will this legislation affect multicultural education?

Historical Developments

Many societies have populations which are ethnically diverse. In European countries, post-war economic expansion brought substantial migration of workers from developing countries. In Britain most of these migrants came from former British colonies. The children of these new citizens entered schools and in the late 1960s several education authorities responded with English language provision. In Bristol, for example, in 1968, an English language teaching service was started, based at the Hannah Moore Primary School. At this stage educationists throughout Britain thought and talked in terms of English for immigrant children. Their underlying conception of their task was one of *integration*, of assimilating these immigrants into 'our' society.

Gradually, however, it was perceived that some children had other 'special' needs relating to their cultural backgrounds. It was also recognized that they had something to offer too. They represented the richness and variety of several major cultural traditions. Attempts were made to develop a multicultural curriculum. All children would learn to celebrate the richness of diversity rather than to fear that which is different.

This move towards a multicultural curriculum has been described as a move from integration to *pluralism*. No longer was the main focus to be on 'fitting' minority ethnic group children into a 'host' society. Rather, all children, indigenous and the British born children of recent immigrants, would receive an education which recognized and valued cultural diversity. This change of focus comes with the recognition that Britain is a multicultural and multiracial society. Most minority ethnic group children are British born. British society, then, should recognize this cultural diversity in its policies and provisions.

Taking Bristol again, as an example, the Hannah Moore language service quickly grew and developed and in 1977 the Multicultural Education Centre was established. Language work was to be part, but not the whole of, the staff's brief. They were also to support schools in the development of a multicultural curriculum. Staff were funded through Section 11 of the 1966 Local Government Act (GB, Home Office, 1966).

Local education authorities, through this Act, were able to seek grant aid to meet up to three quarters of the salary costs of teachers, and others, employed to meet the educational needs of children of 'new commonwealth' (or Pakistani) origin, where these needs are 'different from or additional to' those of indigenous pupils. This Section 11 funding then, was to help to provide for some of the educational needs of particular groups of children. Since these children were mainly living near the centres of large cities, it followed that 'Section 11' funded staff worked in the inner city multiracial schools.

More recently, and in a sense the latest development, is an increasing concern about a variety of race and education issues. Throughout Britain, educationalists are coming to believe that it is not sufficient to incorporate a variety of cultural traditions within the curriculum (important though that is) if we do so within a framework which is itself racially and culturally biased. This move to broaden our concerns has been described as a move from pluralism to *anti-racism*. It has come with the recognition that there are discriminatory structures in the education system which must be recognized and changed; and that teachers need to counter racial bias in learning materials, in the hidden and overt curriculum and in school policies and provisions, (for example, the school's policy on the use of community languages and the school's provision of meals which are culturally acceptable to all the pupils). This involves countering racial prejudices in teacher and pupil attitudes and, even more importantly, changing structures and practices which racially discriminate. Because this racial bias tends to be unintentional, subtle and pervasive, a recent development has been the initiation of racism awareness programmes. The best of these seek to increase a teacher's understanding of how racial prejudice and discrimination function in education, together with increased commitment and ability to develop a more just provision.

These historical developments reveal a widening of perspective. For example, we started with a concern for the special needs of minority ethnic group children. (And, of course, the language and other educational needs of these, as of all children, ought to be catered for.) Then came the recognition that some multicultural education issues are relevant to all children in all schools – issues such as those of racial bias in learning materials and of ethnocentricity in the curriculum. (Unfortunately these important educational needs are not covered by Section 11 funding.)

Similarly, at one time people tended to think of multicultural education as an extra subject, or as a bit of extra content in an existing subject (a project on India, in Geography, for instance), whereas more recently people are thinking in terms of 'permeation'. Multicultural education is seen not as an 'additional bit', but as an aspect of education which should permeate the whole of school life and the child's total educational experience; and all the school staff should be involved, working as a team towards shared objectives. Thus multicultural education is seen to be concerned with the overall ethos, policies, attitudes and objectives of the school as a whole.

Interest in multicultural education is also increasing among people who work at pre-school and post-school stages (nursery teachers and adult education lecturers). Multicultural education issues are felt to be relevant before and after school.

Although these developments have had implications for those concerned with teacher education, provision of both pre-service and of in-service training in multicultural education has been inadequate and even where it has been provided it has often been inappropriate. We will look more closely at the issue of professional development in relation to multicultural education in a later chapter.

In the last few years, thinking about education has been greatly influenced by a major document, the Swann Report, a comprehensive compendium of information, analysis and recommendations relating to multicultural education.

The Swann Report 1985

In 1979 the Government established a committee, under the chairmanship of Anthony Rampton, to enquire into the educational needs and attainment of children from ethnic minority groups, and to make relevant recommendations. In June 1981 this committee published an interim report, *West Indian Children in Our Schools*. The final report, *Education For All* was published in March 1985. Thus this report, commonly known as *The Swann Report* after its new chairman, started out as an inquiry into the education of minority group children, but, after the taking of much evidence from numerous groups and individuals, became concerned with *Education For All*.

The report is very long and expensive. Its eight chapters and various appendices are not likely to be read by more than a minority of busy parents and teachers. Fortunately the Runnymede Trust has produced a useful, concise and accurate summary which is available from the Runnymede Trust (see page 108).

Predictably, the Swann Report has been variously received, but it is clear that the report has been influential and has placed the many issues connected with multicultural education firmly on the educational agenda. It is comprehensive, contains some excellent appendices and recommendations, recognizes the effects of 'institutional racism' (although without much practical guidance on its elimination) and underlines the importance of considering the education of all pupils in a culturally plural society.

The issues it covers include: the ideals of pluralism and education for all, analyses of prejudice and institutional racism, achievement, aspects of language education, religion and the question of separate voluntary aided schools, and teacher education. The final chapter looks at 'other' ethnic minority groups. Three major aspects of multicultural education threaded through the report are language education, the need for a curriculum appropriate for all children and race related concerns.

Language Issues

Britain is not monolingual. Many educationists believe that this ought to be reflected in our education system, and in the school's attitude to linguistic diversity. All children should learn to appreciate the multiplicity of languages and the many interesting forms of a given language.

This is not to deny that competence in Standard English is essential if children are to cope with their school work and if they are later going to be successful in examinations and job interviews. For children whose home language is not English special provision is often made so that they have the opportunity to learn English as a second language quickly and efficiently. Many teachers engaged in this work have had special training and have obtained relevant qualifications, such as the Royal Society of Arts Certificate in the Teaching of English as a Second Language in Multicultural Schools. Increasingly, teachers recognize that Standard English is important for practical reasons, and not because it is linguistically superior to other forms of language. It has been argued, for example, that the principal reason for teaching Standard English in schools is so that children will not be discriminated against for using their own equally good, but lower status, dialects.

West Indian Creoles are often wrongly regarded as 'bad English' and many people working in the multicultural education field ask teachers to recognize that a child's dialect should not be denigrated or belittled, and to encourage pupils to use the wealth and subtle variety of language skills and styles which they possess. A basic knowledge of the main differences between Standard English and West Indian Creoles is useful so that teachers will not assume that a child is making a mistake when s/he is employing a living speech style or dialect. Teachers' lack of knowledge about dialects may hinder the achievements of children of West Indian origin.

Teachers should also recognise the importance of 'mother tongue teaching', of providing, in school, for children whose home language is not English to learn, and sometimes to learn through their first language. The Bullock report (GB. DES, 1975) is often quoted:

> No child should be expected to cast off the language and culture of the home as he crosses the school threshold, nor to live and act as though school and home represent two separate and different cultures which have to be kept firmly apart.

Some young children who attend nursery or infant classes, and who speak little or no English, are hearing and using their mother tongue for some part of the school day. Some secondary school children can choose to learn Panjabi or Urdu or Modern Greek, and so on, up to GCE level.

Multilingual schools, in seeking to cater for all their pupils, may have encountered practical problems because of the range of minority languages involved. Gradually, however, solutions are being found (for example, shared classes for neighbouring schools). Increasingly, too appropriate materials are being developed.

Curriculum Issues

In many secondary schools a multicultural dimension is being developed in all the subjects which may make up the curriculum. This provides for a wider and richer syllabus and is usually intended to have a sensitizing effect on the pupils' developing attitudes to cultural diversity. Those working in the multicultural education field also believe that a young child's education should include some experience of the major cultural traditions that make up our society and should provide opportunities to learn from them. Moreover, children from cultural minority groups need to see that their own languages, religions, lifestyles and histories are recognized and valued by the school.

People learn most effectively if they feel secure and self-confident and this self-confidence is more difficult to achieve for a child to whom school and home seem rigidly separate and mutually alien worlds. In addition, children learn best if their own experience provides a starting point.

There are many reasons, then, for all teachers to reappraise their lessons and check whether this important multicultural dimension has been neglected to the detriment of their pupils. Teachers sometimes work together on this kind of curriculum development.

In literature classes good writers in English from various cultural and racial backgrounds are being selected for study; in drama, children are exploring their own culture and race related experiences and dilemmas; in home economics teachers are incorporating the traditional dishes of a variety of cultural groups; and in religious studies all the major world religions are being included. For many educational institutions religious education has led the way in this multicultural curriculum development. In Birmingham, for example a new agreed syllabus was produced, in 1975, which had a strongly multifaith character and which influenced the curriculum of many schools.

In a number of schools, social studies tutors are beginning to examine, with the children, the topic of race relations in Britain, and at some, appropriate teaching materials have been developed. Even teachers of subjects with a less obvious multicultural dimension (such as maths and science) are learning about the contributions of black peoples and individuals to these fields.

In all secondary school subject areas there has been an increased use of materials, examples, illustrations, contributions, ideas, insights, names and so on, which are not all taken from mainstream white middle-class norms and lifestyles. At the deeper level of the logic of each subject there is increased reference to more than one cultural tradition in seeking to teach its key concepts, truth criteria and procedural principles. Principles of nutrition, for example, can be taught using dishes and diet patterns from a variety of cultural traditions, and aesthetic appreciation can be developed by reference to Kathak or Bharata Natyam dance, as well as to classical ballet; through the appreciation of Caribbean poetry as well as the English Romantics. Examination boards are beginning to reflect these developments within their syllabuses.

Primary school teachers are also developing a multicultural approach to their teaching. One example is the 'multicultural project', in which pupils and teachers explore how common needs and purposes may lie behind a diversity of ways of life – as with the topics of food and dress for example.

Increasingly, too, teachers in schools of all kinds are paying attention to the hidden curriculum – to the unexamined judgements about what is the norm or what constitutes acceptable dress, speech and so on – so that a genuine and unforced multiculturalism begins to permeate the whole of a child's school experience.

This is happening most in multiracial schools, where the need to incorporate a genuine multiculturalism is more obvious and pressing. For example, it may not be sufficient simply to provide multifaith religious education lessons – there is also the daily act of worship to consider, and multifaith religious holidays and festivals to observe.

It is important that a good relationship between these schools and parents should be developed. Much can be achieved through dialogue, including the resolution of apparent culture clash. For example, a Birmingham school, in a series of meetings, reached a mutual agreement with Muslim parents relating to the physical education of their daughters. The parents accepted the need for swimming lessons, on which the school was keen, once they were reassured that the girls changed into their swimming costumes in privacy and were instructed by female staff.

Some schools do all they can to facilitate parental attendance at social occasions and parent evenings by taking into account that many inner city parents have to work unsocial hours; and that some parents do not speak English. Many black parents are concerned that their children are not achieving their academic potential. These parents and many teachers believe that success after school requires the acquisition of the basic skills in reading, writing and arithmetic in the early years, and the development of rigorous academic standards later. Maureen Stone, a black academic, has cautioned that multicultural education could endanger this kind of success.

Ultimately the question of whether multicultural education impedes or enhances education progress and achievement depends upon the conception of 'multicultural education' which one adopts and the educational practices which it entails. The Schools' Council, for example, believes that, correctly interpreted, multicultural education will enhance the attainment of a wide cognitive perspective and the acquisition of intellectual skills:

> A 'good' education should enable a child to understand his own society, and to know enough about other societies to enhance that understanding. A 'good' education cannot be based on one culture only, and in Britain where ethnic minorities form a permanent and integral part of the population, we do not believe that education should seek to iron out the differences between cultures, nor attempt to draw everyone into the dominant culture. On the contrary, it will draw upon the experiences of the many cultures that make up our society and thus broaden the cultural horizons of every child. That is what we mean by 'multicultural education'.

Race Issues

Race issues stem from concerns about racial prejudice and discrimination in education. Many teachers are concerned to counter the racial prejudices of both pupils and of teachers themselves. There is increased awareness of the pervasiveness and influence of racially biased books and learning materials. Moreover, it is claimed that because education has been developed for the white majority, many of our educational policies, provisions and practices are unintentionally racist. These concerns and claims have been strengthened by the findings of the Rampton Report (GB. DES, 1981), that black children are underachieving educationally and that racism is a contributory factor in that underachievement. The Scarman Report (GB. DES, 1982) (of Lord Scarman's inquiry into the Brixton disorders of April 1981) endorsed much of what the Rampton Report had to say on these matters, and recognized that racial discrimination and disadvantage are prevalent in Britain. Many educationists are suggesting that it is because black and white children are growing up in such a society that teachers need an understanding of this and must give race issues a high priority. For example, teachers should know the facts about racial discrimination and disadvantage and should eliminate racial biases from their own teaching. This would involve countering biases, subtle and overt, in school story and text books, in the curriculum, and in the school organization, and devising practices which would remove the disadvantage to minority ethnic groups that currently flaws our education system.

Let us take books as a fairly obvious and specific example. Most books used in schools, fiction and non-fiction, are racially biased. Many are so through omission. In other words they fail to reflect our multiracial and multicultural society and are ethnocentric in assumptions, values and perspectives. Others are biased through commission. They contain stereotyped images of black people, incorrect information about minority ethnic groups and negative attitudes towards ethnic and cultural pluralism. Most are written by white middle class authors and, naturally enough, reflect as the norm, white middle class values and lifestyles.

Children are affected by the images presented to them. Images are powerful attitude formers. This is why teachers should look critically at the books they plan to use, and assess them for racial bias and for damaging negative images or stereotypes.

There are several books which suggest criteria for such assessment, and which encourage teachers to ask themselves such questions as: does the book contain anything which is damaging to the self-esteem of black children, or to the developing racial attitudes of white children, or to the development of a multiracial society? (See page 106.)

The image of the white person as more civilized, law-abiding and generally superior to the black person is a powerful and destructive colonial legacy through which black people have come to be seen, by whites, as 'a problem'. The very presence of black people in Britain is presented as a problem, with a preoccupation about 'how many are here'. The myth of Britain as an overcrowded island has been established. yet more people leave Britain than come to it, most black people who came here were invited when Britain needed labour, and the overwhelming majority of black children in this country were born here and are British. In January 1983 the new Nationality Act (GB. Home Office, 1983) came into force, to add to the preoccupation with the number and status of black people in Britain and to increase the widespread anxiety and insecurity of the black community.

Schools are not immune from this wider picture. They are *of* as well as *in* society. Inevitably they mirror the structures and attitudes of the society of which they are a part. Also inevitably, black children are affected by this racial discrimination and disadvantage – to the detriment of their education and their general life chances. Given the present youth employment situation, it is difficult to hold on to the kind of motivation that academic success demands. As a government survey showed, it takes four times as many interviews for a black school leaver to find a job as for an equivalently qualified white school leaver.

We have now looked, briefly, at some of the main issues of language, curriculum and race, threaded through multicultural education. Recently, important new education legislation has been passed (Education Reform Act 1988, GB. DES, 1988). What are the main provisions and changes proposed by this Act and what are the implications for these important race and culture issues?

ERA (The Education Reform Act) 1988

ERA is the most far-reaching and important education act since 1944. Various parts of the legislation are scheduled to come into force at different stages but its overall impact in the coming years, though not entirely predictable, will certainly be considerable. There are changes in local school management, school and college governing bodies, control of budgets, funding arrangements, power structures and in the curriculum. The major changes are listed below:

1. An end to LEA limits on parents' first choice of schools. (To date each school could not accept pupils above a maximum number set by the LEA. This helped to ensure that all schools had sufficient pupils.)

2. Control of school budgets to be handed over to governors of secondary schools and larger primaries. (Though an LEA 'formula' will control how much total budget each school will receive.)

3. Changes in the composition of school governing bodies.

4. Schools to be allowed to charge for certain activities, for example, evening classes held on school premises.

5. A national curriculum with three compulsory subjects – English, Maths and Science – and seven foundation subjects.

6. Testing for all children at 7, 11, 14 and 16.

7. Religious education to be given special status equal to that of a foundation subject; and a compulsory daily act of collective worship which should be in the main Christian.

8. The ILEA to be abolished and education handed over to the Inner London boroughs.

9. Polytechnics to be established as semi–independent corporations.

10. A University Funding Council to replace the University Grants Committee.

11. A 'Polytechnics and Colleges Funding Council' to administer government funds.

12. Control of further and higher education college budgets to be devolved to governing bodies. Reform of the size and composition of the governing bodies.

All these proposals have given rise to a variety of concerns. Despite a very short time for consultation, the Secretary of State received 1700 responses, most of which seem to have been ignored. The general response of those involved with multicultural education was very critical. ALAOME (The Association of LEA Advisory Officers for Multicultural Education), said that: 'The consultation document fails to display any recognition of ethnic diversity or any appreciation of its educational implications'.

ALAOME expressed concern about several issues: the lack of value placed on concern and respect for others, cooperation and collaboration; that tests as assessment procedures may fail to reflect an ethnically diverse society and thus penalize good work, and that the document neglects the important role of community languages in education, expressed both through bilingual education and the formal teaching of such languages.

The Association's views are summed up in this way:

> To conclude. ALAOME is not opposed to a broad national curriculum *per se*, and believes that there already exists a wide consensus of curriculum practice in schools. Any detailed programme of study drawn up centrally will run the risk of nullifying the freedom of interpretation and delivery which this consultation document promises to protect. Furthermore, we fear that attainment targets, programmes of study and national tests will introduce rigidity rather than flexibility and unless targets programmes and tests are based on principles of multicultural non-racist education, much good practice will wither away. The ignoring of these principles in the consultation document does not give us encouragement.

Such principles, sadly, continued to be ignored in the Act itself.

The implications of the Act then are inequalitarian, running against progress toward more equal opportunities and the Swann Report ideal of a pluralist *Education for All.*

In an editorial of a special issue of FORUM on ERA, the suggestion is made that this Act, which is 'overtly hostile to a multicultural society' is deliberately retrogressive.

By means of this Act the government aims to reverse all the positive and worthwhile educational developments made possible by the 1944 Act. It is vital that governors, parents, teachers, lay and officer members of LEAs understand the intended thrust of this Act. Its malign intent must be thwarted. Its legal framework must be made to deliver a public education service that can be developed to meet the educational needs and aspirations of all. This is the challenge posed by the Education Reform Act to the integrity of everyone involved in the implementation processes.

The question for us then is this. How will the major provision of the Act impact on anti-racist multicultural education, and what loopholes does it contain which provide an opportunity for ensuring that positive and worthwhile progress continues to be made?

ERA and Multicultural Education

1. The national curriculum could become narrowly instrumental, rigid and nationalistic. It is reminiscent of the old grammar school subject centred, competitive approach that is less motivating than more integrated project, theme and collaborative learning approaches for the majority of children, reversing curriculum development of the past 30 years. It is also monolingual. There is no recognition of the importance of linguistic diversity in education.

What are the loopholes or 'windows of opportunity' here? Working parties have been established to draw up a programme of study for each subject (Core and Foundation) and some hope lies here. Moreover, any such programme is open to interpretation by individual teachers who should incorporate an anti-racist pluralist perspective as educationally sound practice. At the time of writing only two groups (maths and science) have produced their programmes, and the science group clearly had access to a pluralist perspective. Where educationalists can influence the groups who are still at work they should do so. Without such influence working parties may unlike the science group, omit cultural diversity. Sadly, the maths group is a case in point.

The science curriculum guidelines, under the heading *Science and Cultural Diversity*, make several key points. Science teachers should be mindful of the needs of pupils who have difficulty with the language of instruction (English). In relation to teacher expectations and the design of learning activities and assessment tasks, care should be taken to avoid ethnic and/or cultural bias. Use should be made of different social contexts for science examples and discussion: for example in relation to diet, nutrition, energy, health and the ecosystem.

The science curriculum must provide opportunities to help all pupils recognize that no one culture has a monopoly of scientific achievement – for example, through discussion of the origins and growth of chemistry from ancient Egypt and Greece to Islamic, Byzantine and European cultures, and parallel developments in China and India. It is important that science books should include examples of people from minority ethnic groups. Pupils should come to realize that the international currency of science is an important force for overcoming racial prejudice.

2. The Act calls for national testing at 7, 11, 14 and 16 years. This could pressure teachers to teach for the tests, and to label many children as failures, with early demotivation, and one wonders how much linguistic and cultural variables will be taken into account. Fortunately the tasks group on attainment and testing, chaired by Paul Black, has produced sensible recommendations. For example: that tests should use a wide range of methods (oral, written, practical) with flexibility: that individual results should be confidential outside discussions between pupils, parents and teachers, but results of the whole class or school should be available to any parent of pupils in the class or school. It has been argued that age related testing could provide realistic and reliable diagnosis of the capabilities of black children. Thus they could become less underestimated than research has shown that, as a group, they are. Clearly the good teacher will have to seek to ensure more accurate assessment of all children – combined with resistance to allowing this recurring testing to damage any child's self-esteem.

3. Another effect of ERA will be to decrease the influence of the Local Education Authority and to increase the responsibility of governing bodies. Yet LEAs have built up some experience in relation to equal opportunities; race, class, gender and disability. (ILEA – The Inner London Education Authority – perhaps the most progressive in this, is, of course, to be destroyed). The loophole here is to seek to influence governors through training, and by finding ways of appointing and co-opting governors with an anti-racist pluralist perspective. For example, ERA's increase in the number of parent governors provides an opportunity for black parents to become more involved in the management of schools.

4. LEAs have traditionally set upper limits on pupil intake each year for each school, in order to ensure a reasonable intake of pupils for them all. ERA abolishes these limits, and also allows schools to opt out of the LEA system altogether. Clearly the tendency will be for a less comprehensive education system, with greater inequality between schools. For example,

greater differences in the social background of pupils will mean greater inequality of parental contributions to financial support.

CHAPTER 2
Theoretical Issues

Before turning to the practice of multicultural education, in this chapter I explore some relevant theoretical issues. What is meant by 'multicultural education', 'anti-racist education' and other key concepts in this field? What are the aims and objectives of multicultural education and how do these relate to other curriculum concerns? The idea of developing a culturally plural curriculum inevitably raises questions about the nature of culturally transmitted beliefs and practices. How can we get a grip on the complex philosophical problem this involves about the nature of knowledge and value? Teachers who have thought through these theoretical issues will feel more confident about what they do in practice and be more able to disentangle confusions and distinguish between positive and tokenistic approaches.

Terminology and Concepts

Terminology

There is an ongoing discussion about what word to use to refer to different ethnic groups. A number of local education authorities have issued advice on this to their employees and a number of books on 'race' list acceptable and unacceptable terms. Some terms are offensive to some people and many teachers are a little anxious about giving offence.

Terminology is both important and unimportant. It is important in that how we feel about things is revealed in the language we use, and language, in turn, can actually influence our deep-seated attitudes. Children are likely to develop negative attitudes towards anything which is consistently talked about in denigratory terms. And if 'race' terms are 'sensitive'this is probably because of the endemic racial prejudices and biased assumptions which our use of language can and does reveal.

Terminology is unimportant in the sense that we cannot just learn to use words by rote from a list of acceptable terms. Language is context dependent and therefore variable and constantly evolving. In any case, it is far more important for us as teachers to think through our own attitudes towards 'other' racial groups and confront and change any stereotypes we may have developed. This increasing awareness of bias will inevitably influence our choice of terms. It is helpful to think about how language conveys implicit messages, but to then use it unselfconsciously. In referring to people by group membership, ask yourself whether their membership of that particular group is actually relevant to the matter in hand. If it is relevant, use the terms members of that group prefer, on the whole, to use themselves.

It might be useful to consider, briefly, the assumptions embedded in a few relevant terms, and to look at some key concepts for anti-racist multicultural education.

Discussion of Terms and Concepts

Race

There are no important biological differences between different ethnic groups. 'Race' is thus a purely social categorization of people based on the tendency for some purely physical characteristics (for example skin tone) to be distinguishable. Many people put 'race' in quotation marks to signify its social rather than its scientific significance.

Immigrants

Most young Afro-Caribbean and Asian people in Britain were born here and are British citizens. It is inaccurate, therefore, to describe them as 'immigrants'. It may also be offensive in that there is an implicit assumption that people are 'foreign' simply by virtue of ethnicity.

Black

This is a political term signifying those groups who suffer discrimination based on their ethnic group. It is not a descriptive term based on skin tone, since some Afro-Caribbean and Asian people are lighter skinned than some Europeans. It tends to be the term preferred by politically aware Afro-Caribbeans and Asians. 'Coloured', by contrast, has colonial and

South African connotations and is disliked by many. In any case, we are all coloured some skin tone or other. White people may use 'coloured' as a euphemism – feeling that to be black is not quite nice. Obviously, used with this undertone the term is offensive! The word 'coloured' tends to be used in white areas more than in multiracial settings. 'Black people' and 'white people' seem to me to be more appropriate ways of referring to human beings than 'blacks' and 'whites', or by exclusion as 'non-whites' and 'non-blacks'
.

Ethnic

We all belong to an ethnic group. Therefore, to talk of 'ethnics' is meaningless. In practice it tends to be used to refer only to minority groups, as though the members of the dominant majority group do not have ethnicity too. With phrases such as 'ethnic dance', are we talking about Indian classical ballet or some combination of the many forms of dance from several cultural traditions? We can be more accurate about what we mean. Where we wish to refer to all the minority groups we can use 'minority ethnic groups'. ('Ethnic minority groups' again subtly carries the implicit idea that only minority groups are ethnic!)

Special needs

This phrase is so well-entrenched in our educational vocabulary that it is difficult to avoid. What we should be aware of is that many so called special needs are not special at all. They are the educational needs of any child. For example, we talk of learning one's home language as being a 'special'need. Yet clearly it is a need that all children share. We talk of learning English as a second language as being a special need. Of course children whose first language is not English do need to learn English – again as any child in this society must. To learn English or any other language as a *second* language is surely only 'special' in an educational system which is linguistically impoverished.

We should also be aware that the term 'special need' is used completely differently in connection with the 1981 Education Act (GB. DES, 1981) concerning special education. The 1981 Education Act use of 'special need' is connected with the concept of learning difficulties. Black children, as a group, do not have learning difficulties, though, as with children from the white indigenous group, a proportion of them do. Sadly, some black children are wrongly thought to be slow learners because what has been assessed is not their learning ability or conceptual level, but merely their competence in standard English.

Racial Prejudice

In Chapter 2 of the Swann Report (GB. DES, 1985) an analysis of prejudice is provided. Prejudice is defined as a preconceived opinion or bias for or against someone or something, where the opinion has been formed without adequate information on which to base a rational judgement. Such judgements are often directed against groups of people who are assumed to share common attributes and behaviour patterns. Racial prejudice thus requires that we have formed a stereotype of a particular group of people, which then allows one to judge a member of this group according to an established set of expectations. The two factors essential for racial prejudices initially to be formed and then maintained are:

- ignorance;

- the existence and promulgation of stereotypes of particular groups of people are conveyed by the media and by the education process.

This brief helpful account of prejudice shows how it goes beyond simple prejudgement, through the connection with stereotyping, and bringing out that racial prejudices are reinforced and legitimated through the media and through education.

What could be added to this Swann analysis? Prejudice rests on irrational beliefs which *are* irrational because there is an emotional resistance to changing them. They do not change in the light of new evidence. Indeed/evidence is distorted to fit in with the prejudice. Moreover, prejudice influences one's behaviour. Racial prejudices are expressed in hostile actions which tend to escalate. As W.H. Allport (1958) found, in his comprehensive study of prejudice, there is a tendency to move along a continuum from antilocution (verbal abuse) through to physical attack (or even genocide). We can therefore add two more factors to Swann's original two, namely:

- emotional investment in the irrational beliefs;

- the expression of the prejudice in harmful discriminatory behaviour.

Racial Discrimination

Racial discrimination occurs when a person is unfairly treated (because s/he is a member of a particular racial group) relative to more favourable treatment of persons in a different racial group. The difference in treatment is harmful and unjustifiable; based solely on racial grounds.

Institutional Racism

The Swann Report describes this as the way in which a range of long established systems, practices and procedures in education and the wider society, which were originally devised to meet the needs of a relatively homogeneous society, may unintentionally work against minority groups by depriving them of opportunities open to the majority group. Examples of such unintended discrimination would include:

1. School assemblies which provide only Christian forms of worship – failing to cater for an assembly of children from homes which include a range of religious traditions. (Unfortunately, ERA will encourage this discrimination since it stipulates that the act of worship should, in the main, be broadly Christian.)

2. Providing school dinner which some groups of children cannot eat for religious/cultural reasons – failing to offer a range of choices such that all pupils can receive a nutritious midday mean.

3. Language practices which disadvantage children and families whose home language is not English, for example:

   (a) Notes and letters home only in English.

   (b) Teaching community languages only in lunchtime or after school.

   (c) Mistaking a pupil's lack of competence in standard English for lack of ability.

   (d) Failing to recognize bi- or multilingualism as educationally advantageous.

This emphasis on unintentional discrimination within institutional practices and procedures is important because, though widespread, it is often unrecognized. Of course racial discrimination by the powerful group, in some circumstances, is deliberate – whether openly so or unadmitted.

Pluralism

In recommending pluralism in education, one means more than mere recognition that our society contains a plurality of cultures and ethnic groups. Rather it represents an idea or ideal of equality of standing for these various groups. (Not everyone, of course, shares this ideal.)

Educational Aims and Objectives

When, as teachers, we ask ourselves about our educational aims, we are asking a fundamental question about what we are ultimately seeking to achieve through the activities in which we engage our pupils. What is the point of what we are going to do on Monday morning? In a sense this is to ask ourselves what our conception of *education* is, because to ask about the purpose or point of educational activities is equivalent to asking about the nature of education. When we have worked out our fundamental aims we can then work our smaller steps along the way – the objectives of particular learning activities. Traditionally these terms, 'aims' and 'objectives', have been used in this way – to distinguish between the fundamental, long term purposes of education (aims) and the smaller, achievable goals (objectives) which constitute progress towards these broader ends.

There is a considerable literature within the Philosophy of Education, about the concept of education. Three key points in this discussion are:

1. Education is about developing desirable qualities in pupils.

2. Education develops a 'wide cognitive perspective'.

3. Education promotes autonomy.

These are aspects of liberal education. A more radical concept also involves the notion of education as social action – as the means by which a society maintains the status quo or through which it can, to lesser or greater degrees, change the society in which it takes place. Preserving the status quo tends to correlate with a transmissionist view of knowledge – we pass on knowledge and values which remain unchanged. To seek to change society through education tends to correlate with a transformationist view of knowledge – we equip pupils to be critical and to transform existing beliefs into new perspectives.

At the individual level education necessarily involves change, for no one is educated who remains just as s/he was. Thus, education is inescapably normative. It involves our value judgements about what changes should be sought.

Not just any worthwhile change counts as educational. A child may, for example, be trained to respond, unthinkingly, in certain useful ways. We talk of potty training, not of potty education. Worthwhile educational changes involve the development of knowledge (including knowing how to do complex tasks skilfully) and understanding. Such knowledge and understanding as 'widen our horizons', 'open doors', 'enable and empower', 'fulfil our potential' and 'develop critical minds' ... etc. These commonly heard phrases suggest, in the words of R.S. Peters, that the kind of knowledge and understanding involved in education will promote a 'wide cognitive perspective' in our apprehension of the world.

To develop this kind of broad understanding of our experiences enables us to arrive at rational opinions of our own and to make informed decisions about our own lives. Many educationalists see the attainment of such autonomy as the basic educational aim.

It is surely not possible to *seriously* work towards these kinds of liberal education ends and to choose a monocultural and ethnocentric approach. They must involve unbiased knowledge and understanding of the various cultural traditions and ethnic groups within our own society and in the world of which it is a part.

Moreover, if children are to be prepared, as adults, to bring about and function in a *just* multi-ethnic society, this has implications for the kinds of values which will inform our educational ideals. As we have seen, education can never be value neutral – and the values built into 'education for a multicultural society' are those of justice, equality, artistic and intellectual freedom, freedom for cultural diversity, and the valuing of this diversity itself.

Actually even a purely instrumental, vocational and narrow conception of education, as being only to prepare children for work, could also incorporate a multicultural perspective. Children learning in 'all white' areas of Britain may later work in more multiracial settings and should (pragmatically) have some understanding of groups other than their own.

Education broadly conceived is about developing rational beliefs rather than prejudices, about developing critical faculties and moral qualities and commitments in our pupils and about developing their autonomy. Schooling that is ethnocentric and biased, monocultural and narrow, and which is unconcerned about children's attitudes and values *must* be *miseducation.*

The humanizing values and ideals implicit in multicultural education are also embedded in moral education, personal and social education and development education. An 'education' that neglected to teach children to act rightly for right reasons and to respect other people; or that neglected the personal and social development of each pupil, or that failed to provide a global perspective in their understanding of our interdependent world would, again, be miseducation. In terms of their values, and their concerns about pupils' attitudes to themselves and to other people and groups of people, all these important aspects of education interrelate.

What is Multicultural Education?

The term multicultural education is widely used and has been both contrasted with anti-racist education and joined to it ('Anti-racist multicultural education'). Some teachers feel wary of it, whatever it is, because it seems to be surrounded by controversy and to mean different things to different people. A teacher is best equipped to ideal with controversy if she was worked out for herself what she means by multicultural education and what she believes is educationally sound. I want to explore some of these meanings of 'multicultural education', then turn to 'anti-racist education and the relationship between these two. My own contention is that there *is* such a relationship, and that the issues associated with anti-racist multicultural education are too important for us to ignore.

It is not possible to give one short, clear, universally acceptable definition of 'multicultural education'. Given the variety of conceptions of 'education' and the similarly wide variety of possible definitions of 'culture', this lack of a simple or universally agreed definition is hardly surprising.

Because these are various conceptions of multicultural education, people who all claim to want it may nevertheless disagree about what should actually happen in schools. They are operating with very different aims and with differing concerns. One could say, then, that 'multicultural education' is an umbrella term, used to refer to a variety of approved or demanded practices in educational establishments. These are practices such as mother tongue teaching, the provision of 'ethnic' school dinners, the elimination of ethnocentricity in history, the inclusion of non-Christian religions in school assembly, and so on. Which of these practices a given individual approves of reveals an implicit concept of multicultural education, arising from specific concerns.

A number of practices stem from a concern for the special needs of minority ethnic group children. 'English as a second language' is an example of this. Other practices may follow from a concern about race relations in Britain. The elimination of racial bias in books and other learning materials would be an example here. A broad conception of multicultural education incorporates several interrelated concerns and generates many practical implications.

Similarly, the various perspectives on multicultural education which have been identified in the past could be seen as closely interrelated and subsumed within one broad all-embracing conception.

These perspectives included an *equality of opportunity* perspective, which involves provision to compensate for underachievement; the *individual and group fulfilment* perspective, which entails the development of language skills and the discussion of social issues such as prejudice and discrimination; and the *social and political justice* perspective, which requires remedy for alienation through the provision of 'black studies' or 'mother tongue teaching'. Though these three models have been distinguished in the literature one could, it seems to me, see any one of them as entailing the educative provision subsumed under both of the other two.

There are a number of new ways in which one might attempt to distinguish and clarify some of these many conceptions of multicultural education. One could, for example, take the more commonly accepted analyses of 'education' and ask for each one – 'Given this analysis of "Education" what might be meant by "multicultural education"?'. Thus an account of education that stressed the development of autonomy might lead one of the view that genuine choice among different ways of life and world views presupposes knowledge of them.

Education is often explicated in terms of the development of rationality. In the context of multicultural education this, as I have pointed out, leads us to consider the nature of rational thought. If there are standards of rationality which are culture context dependent, children could only come to understand these various forms of rationality through initiation into a variety of cultures.

A more direct approach is to put the initial emphasis on 'multicultural' rather on 'education' by asking what might be meant by *multicultural* education. Three interpretations emerge:

1. Education through many cultures.

2. Education in many cultures.

3. Education for a multicultural society.

'Multicultural education' is sometimes used to mean education 'through' many cultures in the sense that the educative process makes use of multicultural elements. Education is brought about through the use of these elements. Obviously just which elements are selected and how and why they are to be presented will depend upon the particular conception of education involved. Education 'in' several cultures encompass the idea that cultural traditions embody distinctive worthwhile knowledge and forms of thought. A monocultural education would, therefore, deprive children of much that is of value and interest. This means that there are logical reasons for regarding a comprehensive education as necessarily multicultural. Children, including minority ethnic group children, move from an understanding of their own experience (linguistic, religious, etc) to a more complete understanding of the wider world. And a (relatively) complete aesthetic, or religious, or linguistic education must involve a range of cultural traditions. There are *moral* imperatives connected with the idea of educating children for a *just* multicultural society.

We can see that a *broad* conception of multicultural education incorporates a wide range of issues and points to the necessity of a culturally plural curriculum for all children. Whatever this entails in practice we are clearly not dealing with superficial optional extras in the curriculum. This kind of practice has been dubbed the three 'S's' approach – the addition of 'saris, samosas and steel bands' to school life. The practice we will seek to develop should reflect a more fundamental valuing of cultural diversity. The curriculum should incorporate a variety of cultural traditions in such a way that the teachers basic educational aims and objectives are achievable; aims and objectives which have themselves been formulated with regard to our multicultural society.

What is Anti-Racist Education?

The previous section of this chapter was concerned with cultural pluralism in the curriculum. Multicultural education (education 'in' and 'through' several cultures) is about eliminating ethnocentricity from our teaching by getting rid of ethnic bias from lesson content, teaching approaches and learning materials. The curriculum is permeated by a culturally plural dimension.

Increasingly, educationalists are realizing that such pluralism could, and largely has, left untouched the deep-seated racial prejudices of teachers and pupils and the large scale and unfair discrimination built into the education system itself. It is not always easy or palatable for white teachers to recognize this radial prejudice and see it clearly for what it is. Nor are we aware of how consistently educational policies and practices discriminate against (often unintentionally) members of minority ethnic groups, particularly black groups. Some examples of such institutional discrimination were given earlier in this chapter. Because of this endemic prejudice and discrimination there is a growing recognition of the need for education against such racism.

An 'anti-racist' education will, therefore, aim to counter both racial discrimination and racial prejudice. It will be many-faceted because discrimination occurs at all levels of the system; for example, from LEA and school recruitment procedures, to individual teacher/pupil relationships. Anti-racist education will be concerned with teacher education to change our prejudiced attitudes, which are often influenced by stereotypes and expressed in low expectations of black pupils.

It will also aim to develop unprejudiced attitudes and values in pupils. This has implications for the hidden as well as the overt curriculum. A teacher influences pupils through unthinking assumptions and comments as well as by what she actually teaches about 'race' related matters. Teaching may be directly about 'racism', or, more often, indirectly about it, in geography, history, religion, etc. The curriculum aspects of anti-racist education overlap with 'education for a multicultural society', and is a significant part of each pupil's personal and social development.

Anti-racist education is important. The term 'multicultural education' has the wider coinage, but it must be emphasized that educational issues involve 'race' as well as culture; the elimination of structural discrimination as well as of pupils' prejudices. In order to incorporate all these aspects the use of the rather cumbersome phrase 'anti-racist multicultural education' has emerged.

Anti-Racist Multicultural Education

This phrase 'anti-racist multicultural education' has also partly grown out of relatively recent debates in which multicultural education and anti-racist education have been presented as alternatives For example, the Spring 1985 issue of *Multicultural Teaching* draws attention to the then current discussions about the putative dichotomy between multicultural and anti-racist education. In his article in that journal, Robin Grinter argues that we need to bridge the gulf between them (Grinter, 1985). He points out that multiculturalists 'hope to educate for understanding and appreciation of the diversity of life styles that make up our society' and thereby to weaken the hold of 'prejudices which combine and sustain discriminatory behaviour. Academics such as Chris Mullard and Hazel Carby, on the hand, had dismissed this multicultural approach as superficial and irrelevant, and 'a right-wing inspired sop to communities who are suffering injustices both in social/economic and in cultural terms'.

In a subsequent issue of the aforementioned journal I argued that there need be no gulf between multicultural and anti-racist education; that multicultural education ought to be anti-racist and that anti-racist education must be (in one sense of the term) 'multicultural', to combat cultural racism.

Chris Mullard had claimed that anti-racist education rests on a sound theoretical basis and that multicultural education does not. He distinguished between the structure of the education system and the cultural content of the curriculum. This distinction reminds us that education has both organizational and substantive aspects. The structures by which education is organized and administered are often unfairly discriminatory and Chris Mullard is right to highlight this and to give it priority. But the content of the curriculum, the substantive aspect of education with which teachers are directly concerned, can be biased too. It is here that the dichotomy between anti-racist education on the one hand, and multicultural education on the other, is, I think, mistakenly introduced.

Mullard equates anti-racist education with structure, and multicultural education with content, and sees them as alternative forms of 'racial education'. However, it is because multicultural education is concerned with curriculum content, and in so far as that content is anti-racist, that multicultural education is anti-racist education too. Of course, whenever the content of multicultural education is not functioning against racism, it cannot be equated with anti-racist education in this way. The point is that it is not anti-racist education and multicultural education that are alternative forms of education, but that there are alternative forms of multicultural education – racist (R) and anti-racist (AR) forms. Unlike the racist forms, the anti-racist form of multicultural education is not an alternative to anti-racist education but a part of it.

It is easy to mistake R for AR. However, we cannot let this deter us from developing a multicultural curriculum since to do so is to miseducate. Rather we need to understand the difference between genuine pluralism (AR) and tokenist multiculturalism (R). Aspects of this difference between positive (anti-racist) and negative (racist) curriculum development will become clearer later in this chapter and when we look at exam

Table 1: Analysis of Racist Education and Anti-Racist Education

ANTI-RACIST EDUCATION	
STRUCTURES	*CONTENT*
Non-discriminatory policies and practices for equality of outcomes	Genuine pluralism in the curriculum
	Anti-racist teaching including teaching about racism

RACIST EDUCATION	
STRUCTURES	*CONTENT*
Discriminatory policies and practices	Tokenist pluralism in the curriculum
Underachievement	Mono-cultural ethnocentric education

ples, in *practice*, of each. In the meantime, Table 1 above illustrates the relationship between forms of multiculturalism and anti-racist education.

Curriculum Development and Cultural Relativism

The nature of knowledge

Earlier in the chapter we saw that 'multicultural education' involves the notion of developing a curriculum which is in some way culturally plural, containing knowledge and values drawn from more than one cultural tradition. Because we are concerned with *education* the knowledge must be genuine knowledge (that is, not superstition, or guesswork or prejudice). It must also be worthwhile (that is, of value). How are we to select this knowledge? Does all knowledge derive from correct principles of human thought which are universal – embedded in all cultural traditions? These rational principles would provide the platform (the criteria of selection) from which we as educators, could, without ethnocentricity, make our culturally plural curriculum selection. Or, does all (or some) knowledge derive from principles of rationality which are culture relative? If rationality is culture bound in this way, whose principles should be used for curriculum selection?

These questions are connected to long-standing philosophically important problems in epistemology, ethics and metaphysics. What is the nature of knowledge and rationality? From where do values derive and are they (and if so in what sense) objective? Does a culture transcendent reality partly determine rational thought about it or do a range of socially constructed conceptual schemes embody various context dependent realities?

It is apparent that the idea of a multicultural curriculum raises complex theoretical issues by inescapably posing the question: Is knowledge necessarily what it is and therefore cross cultural, or is knowledge socially constructed and therefore culturally variable?

We could answer this question in any one of three ways.

- Knowledge is a universal 'given', which transcends cultural traditions (absolutism).

- Knowledge is socially constructed, and completely culture relative (cultural relativism).

- Knowledge is socially constructed; there are some universal aspects of such constructs and some culture relative aspects (limited relativism).

In what follows I have set out each of these answers more fully, and indicated what follows for each as far as multicultural education is concerned. It is important to grasp the problem and to understand these possible answers to it because the differences between them make significant differences in our approach to the practice of multicultural education.

The Absolutist Position

The absolutist believes that there are principles of thought (and value judgements) which any group of human beings must use if they are to be fully rational (and fully moral). Let us call this thesis that there are overarching culture free principles of rationality 'absolutist'!

Absolutists have argued (1) that complete relativism would entail maintenance of the dominant culture or culture apartheid, since we would have

no cross-cultural principles by which to develop a non-ethnocentric curriculum for all children in a multicultural society. Absolutists have also
argued (2) that if relativism were true we could not even identify another
culture's beliefs. However, we do have to be initiated into our own culture before we can identify beliefs pertaining to it as beliefs. In principle
then, could we not also come to identify beliefs embedded in a very different framework of concepts and with different truths criteria?

There are telling logical arguments against both absolutism and relativism, which is why the debate has continued, in one form or another vir-
tually since philosophy began. Absolutism and Relativism are in a kind
of 'mirror image difficulty'. The relativist on his own terms cannot claim
to state an objective (that is culture transcendent) truth, while the absolutist does claim to do so, but can speak only from within his own system.

Although in this logical or philosophical sense there is little to choose
between absolutism or cultural relativism, in terms of implication in practice for multicultural education, there are three grave educational implications associated with the absolutist position.

1.   If we accept absolutism, we have to accept that because a mono-
      cultural education could introduce pupils to all the principles of
      rationality, education *need* not be multicultural. This could
      encourage one aspect of racism in education viz. the neglect of
      minority cultures.

2.   An absolutist tends to assume that his own cultural laws of thought
      and value judgements are *the* valid laws of thought and *the* valid
      value judgements and that 'other' culture ways of thought and
      value system deviate from them. This encourages ethnocentricity.

3.   A teacher with absolutist assumptions accepts that there is one set
      of absolute truths (facts and values) and picks and chooses from
      several cultural traditions only at the level of lesson content and
      learning materials. She uses this material from several cultures to
      illuminate the supposedly cross-cultural universals. This neglects
      the deeper procedural level. There is no culturally plural develop-
      ment at the level of the logic of the various forms of knowledge
      and their culture relative key concepts, truth criteria and values.

Thus, as we will see in the next chapter, in actual examples, when we
look at these three educational implications in terms of classroom practice, absolutist assumptions tend to lead to a tokenist approach to multiculturalism. Superficial cultural features are integrated into a lesson

whose deeper assumption and values remain always rooted in the dominant culture. This may well foster attitudes that the teacher does not intend regarding the relative importance of these 'other' cultures. Such tokenistic pluralism does not counter racism but actually reinforces it. It reinforces the tendency to regard the dominant culture as the norm from which others deviate. The tendency to elevate the dominant group's forms of thought values as 'transcendentally' correct can be discerned. From the perspective provided by these culture-relative principles, other cultures are surveyed. One tends to judge one's own system as more valid than the systems of others. (Given relativism, one can see why this should be so. According to criteria internal to one's own system they simply are correct.) Let us then look more closely at the relativist position.

The Relativist Position

The cultural relativist believes that there could be, and are, different and yet equally valid principles of thought for different groups of human beings; that there are no absolute culture-free principles of rationality; and that the imposition of culture bound principles represents the imposition of the dominant group's culture. Let us call this thesis that principles of rationality are culture bound 'cultural relativism'. (The thesis is more than that different cultures, as a matter of *fact* have different principles. This might mean only that some groups have irrational principles. Rather, different cultural traditions embody different yet equally *valid* principles.)

The cultural relativist is sometimes accused of subjectivism; of believing that any principle is acceptable; that, for example, fascist principles are, on this thesis, as rational or moral as anti-racist ones. However, cultural relativism does not entail that principles are based on mere preference or arbitrary decisions. There are rules and 'necessities' intersubjectively agreed because they are appropriate to certain human needs and purposes. Because the many forms of dance may each have distinct aesthetic principles does not entail that these aesthetic principles have been arbitrarily chosen or that others would have served equally well.

Unlike absolutism, the relativist position entails that a *complete* education must be multicultural. A monocultural education arbitrarily excludes perfectly valid forms of thought. Moreover, unlike absolutist assumption through which one tends to judge one's own thought perspectives as more valid than the system of others, relativism provides the insight that 'other' systems could be equally valid. Such an insight will have an effect on the pupil's attitude to cultural diversity and to 'other' ways of living, belief systems and value judgements, without weakening the pupil's affective commitment to those she chooses for her own.

The disadvantage with relativism lies in its implication of the lack of any shared criteria for curriculum selection across cultural boundaries and the similar lack of shared values, even, presumably, the sharing of the values which are inherent in the ideals of multicultural education itself. For example, the Swann Report (GB. DES, 1985) advocates cultural pluralism within a common framework of values which members of all ethnic groups share. If complete cultural relativism is valid, there would be no such common framework.

What we need is a theoretical position which would both allow the possibility of some shared, universal principles and values, and some culturally relative ones. This would provide the best of both worlds. We would avoid the tokenism and cultural imperialism of absolutist perspectives. We would retain the idea of diversity at the deeper procedural level of the curriculum. We would encourage the tolerance born of the relativistic insight previously mentioned. In other words, we could recognize the value of a diversity of 'other' perspectives and yet, recognize a common framework of values. This framework also provides the criteria to distinguish between perspectives (and ways of life, value systems, and so on) and to select and to reject.

The third position, 'limited relativism', avoids many of the philosophical problems associated with complete absolutism and complete relativism. It also provides a good theoretical basis for a sound approach to an anti-racist multicultural education. 'Limited relativist' assumptions, as we will see, retains the advantages while avoiding the disadvantages (for anti-racist multicultural education) associated with the two more philosophically extreme positions.

Limited Relativism

For the limited relativist there are some shared principles of rational thought and some shared values which co-exist with and are influenced (and influence) many unshared, culture specific but nevertheless valid ones. (For our purposes it is irrelevant why the shared principles are necessarily applicable to all groups.) Stephen Lukes has given an account of such a limited relativist position in his paper 'Some problems about rationality' (Lukes, 1974). He suggests that some criteria of rationality are universal, that is, they are relevantly applicable to all beliefs in any context, and some are context dependent, that is, they are to be discovered by investigating the context and are only relevantly applicable to beliefs in that context. He calls the former 'rational (1) criteria' and the latter, context-dependent criteria, 'rational (2) criteria'. With this philosophical position, education both into and through other cultures is important. We need to be educated into several cultural traditions if we are to come to understand a variety of rational (2) criteria of rationality, and in the sense that we know a place better if we approach it from many directions we will better understand the universal criteria of rationality – rational (1) – if we have the advantage of several contexts, that is through several cultures.

Peter Winch also adopted a limited relativist position in his paper 'Understanding a primitive society' (Winch, 1958). He pointed out that there are certain limiting concepts which will be important to any human society or in any life (birth, death, sexual relations) and that conceptual schema are not isolated and insulated because they are all unified in being part of a person's life. He went on to say:

> What we may learn by studying other cultures are not merely possibilities of different ways of doing things, other techniques. More importantly we may learn different possibilities of making sense of human life, different ideas about the possible importance that the carrying out of certain activities may take on for a man, trying to contemplate the sense of his life as a whole.

A Common Framework of Values

We started with an ideal – of an education appropriate for a multicultural society. From this we recognized the need for developing an anti-racist multicultural curriculum for all children in common (that is non-segregated) schools. Clearly, if educationist not to mean cultural domination by the most powerful group (an ethnocentric curriculum) then the minority groups must have an equal voice in that curriculum development; if those educationalists and parents who share this pluralist ideal are to approve the curriculum consequently developed (whatever their cultural/ethnic background) then it must be developed within a framework of beliefs and values which they all share.

One is in a different dialogue with those who for whatever reason reject the pluralist ideal. Those who wish to impose on all children their own absolutist view (of whichever group) rather than promoting autonomy, tolerance and dialogue, or those who wish to impose a biased view, preferring ethnocentricity, have a different conception of 'education'. The limited relativism which we have found to underpin pluralism must be joined to liberal values, because without such values cultural pluralism in education becomes impossible.

There is currently much talk about British values and the British Cultural Heritage. Such phrases are even enshrined in the new Education Reform Act (GB. DES, 1988). But what precisely are British values or the British culture? Is this excluding the cultural traditions of minority groups from 'British Culture' and black people from being 'British'? There is danger here of perpetuating racist myths and assumptions. There is no static monolithic British culture. Cultures are dynamic and many stranded. British society is constituted of a plurality of changing ways of life, languages, art forms, religion and so on just as British citizens are of many kinds.

The Swann Report (GB. DES, 1985) also worked with this notion of cultural diversity within 'a common framework of values'. (It is not clear if the report presumes we already have such a framework or must construct it.) The report's recommendations are based on the idea of educating all children, from whatever ethnic group, to an understanding of the shared values of society as a whole as well as to an appreciation of the diversity of lifestyles and cultural, linguistic and religious backgrounds which make up this society and the wider world. In so doing, all pupils should be given the knowledge and skills needed, not only to contribute positively to shaping the future nature of British society, but also to determine their own individual identities.

Educational philosophers John White and Graham Haydon (1987) have provided some suggestions about how we might construct our common framework of values. White feels that in addition to whatever shared values we already have, we need to work out what out common values should be and sees this as an on-going unending *collective activity* of society as a whole, setting about the task of 'collective self-understanding about our values'. Haydon sees the education process as itself providing a forum for the *negotiation* of the framework of values for society as a whole.

White also suggests that increasingly there would be a convergence on values which lie closest to our common human nature as social, symbol-using animals conscious of our morality. My own belief is similar. If children are initiated into a variety of conceptual schemas, in making comparisons between and in synthesizing from them there will tend to be substantial agreement in their judgements. For shared understandings to be possible, human response must manifest a broad agreement. It is not over-optimistic, then, to assume that a pluralist education for all children in common schools will produce citizens who have considerable freedom and variety of choice in their life-styles, languages, cultural activities, religions and so on and exercise this freedom within a substantial shared framework of common beliefs and basic values which emerge for most children educated in such a way.

In any case, once we accept the pluralist ideas of an education appropriate (and playing a part in creating) an open society in which there is equality of status between different cultural and ethnic groups, then we have already accepted a number of fundamental values and guiding principles. This idea rests on the democratic liberal values of equality and justice, the celebration of diversity and tolerance of 'other' views and lifestyle. Individuals must be free to debate, criticize and disagree.

Equality and justice underpin, as we have seen, the issues relating to anti-racist education combating both intentional and unintentional discrimination to provide more genuine equality of opportunity, and, therefore, more equality of outcomes for minority groups. The celebration of diversity, with understanding of and respect for 'other' cultures, is implicit in the idea of developing a genuinely plural curriculum. Democratic values are also implicit in multicultural education and find practical expression at many levels: including pupil/teacher relationships, non-hierarchical approaches to school organization, genuine consultation with parents and participation in decision making by parents and children.

Analytic Models

Let us sum up the points made about cultural relativism and multicultural education.

Absolutism

Advantage – Allows for a common framework of shared rational principles and values.

Disadvantage – Absolutist presuppositions can lead to a monocultural education; the neglect of minority cultures. Where multicultural elements are used they tend to be at a superficial, tokenistic level because 'other' cultures are approached from the perspective of the dominant culture. (For example, a Christian perspective of Divali: the Festival of Lights presented as 'The Hindu Christmas').

Relativism

Advantage – Relativism shows why monocultural education is incomplete – neglecting valid 'other' forms of knowledge; it provides the insight that diversity contains richer possibilities of knowledge and value.

Disadvantage – Relativism does not allow a common framework of rational principles and values by which agreed curriculum for comprehensive pluralist schools could be constructed.

Limited Relativism

This position contains the advantages of both the above positions; it avoids their disadvantages.

Absolutist and relativist conception of multicultural education correlate with ideas about the purpose of multicultural education, which are discernible in the multicultural/anti-racist debate previously discussed. The 'conservative' wing (integrationists) see multicultural education as being an education which draws, for material, on minority cultures, but which essentially leaves everything as it is. The 'liberal' wing see multicultural education as being an education into cultural tradition. The 'radical' wing concentrate on changing the structures of the education system to provide equality (of outcome) for all children, regardless of race, class or gender, growing up in multicultural Britain.

Table 2 sets out these three 'models' of multicultural education. Model 2 and model 3 are mutually supportive. Unlike model 1, model 2 does not apprehend 'other cultures' from a vantage point anchored in the dominant culture. Model 3 is equivalent to model 2 (a non tokenist multicultural curriculum) plus the demand for anti-racist structures.

There is a racist conception of multicultural education (model 1) and an anti-racist conception (model 2). Anti-racist multicultural education (model 2) is necessary, but not sufficient, for full anti-racism in education (model 3). It is necessary because anti-racism demands genuine pluralism in the curriculum; for example, in terms of the development of pupil attitudes to a plural society and in terms of exposure to alternative perspectives. It is insufficient for anti-racist education because anti-racism must address the issue of structural discrimination too. Table 3 illustrates the relationship between models of multicultural education and anti-racist education.

Table 2: Models of Multicultural Education

MODEL	FACTION	CONCEPTION	ISSUES	METAPHYSIC
1. Education THROUGH Several Cultures	CONSER-VATIVE	ABSOLUTIST	INTEGRATION e.g. E2L, Cultural tokenism	ABSOLUTISM
2. Education IN Several Cultures	LIBERAL	RELATIVIST	PLURALISM e.g. Community languages, Curriculum Pluralism	RELATIVISM & LIMITED RELATIVISM
3. Education FOR a Multi-cultural Society	RADICAL	MORAL/ ANTI-RACIST	ANTI-RACISM e.g. Elimination of discrimination and equality of outcome	LIMITED RELATIVISM

Table 3: Models of Multicultural Education and Anti-Racist Education

ANTI-RACIST EDUCATION

Anti-racist Education MODEL 3	STRUCTURES	CONTENT	Anti-racist Multicultural Education MODEL 2
	Non-discriminatory policies and practices for Equality of Outcomes	Genuine pluralism in the curriculum	Anti-racist Multicultural Education MODEL 2
		Anti-racist teaching including teaching about race	MODEL 3

RACIST EDUCATION

STRUCTURES	CONTENT	Racist Multicultural Education MODEL 1
Discriminatory policies and practices	Tokenist pluralism in the curriculum	Racist Multicultural Education MODEL 1
Underachievement	Monocultural ethnocentric education	Most current British Education

In this chapter we have looked at many theoretical issues connected with multicultural education. Some of these are philosophically complex. It will not be surprising if non-philosophers have found the discussion a bit heavy going. The key points to take from it are:

a) Educators cannot draw on all that is worthwhile if they are restricted to one cultural tradition.

b) To understand just one cultural tradition and judge others from this limited perspective leads to ethnocentricity.

c) Those who accept the liberal democratic values built into the idea of education for a pluralist society (and accordingly allow all groups a voice in the task) should be able to construct a framework of values which will provide guidance in constructing an education appropriate for all children in a just, multiethnic Britain.

We must go on to consider how this theory can be translated into practice. Key theoretical principles for anti-racist multicultural education, when cashed out in practical terms, will provide guidance for our classroom activities.

In the next chapter, I shall give concrete examples of the different analytic models of multicultural education. We shall see examples of what not to do – the negative approach of model 1; and examples of the positive approaches of both developing an anti-racist multicultural curriculum (model 2) and of anti-racist education (model 3).

Part ll
FROM THEORY TO PRACTICE

CHAPTER 3
Theory, Practice and Change

Theory and Practice Related

Theory, without a grounding in what is possible in practice, is empty; practice without theoretical guidance is blind. Teachers need to develop their classroom practice within a wider understanding of educational theory and enrich that theoretical understanding in the light of reflection on their practical experience.

Such an ongoing relationship between theory and practice is what is meant by 'praxis'. Theory is not, as in science, a logically connected set of hypotheses which explain the phenomena of educational practice. Rather 'educational theory' refers both to a general philosophy of education and also to complex interdisciplinary thinking which guides action. The former provides a framework of understanding for our practice and the latter has a bearing on the solution of practical problems. This thinking to guide action incorporates general practical principles which are justified by their validity within various relevant disciplines (for example psychology and sociology) and beliefs and values.

The reflections in Chapter 2 provide both a framework for understanding education (an anti-racist multicultural perspective) and some guidance for action in terms of criteria for distinguishing between developments which are genuinely anti-racist and pluralist, from those which are not. Let us look more explicitly at the guidance for educational practice that Chapter 2 can provide. What considerations emerged from that discussion which should inform and guide our classroom activities?

1. It emerged from a consideration of language use and terminology that our assumptions, values and attitudes are reflected even in the language we use. We know, as teachers, that much our pupils learn from us is 'caught not taught'. How can we be good teachers in terms of the subtle messages which we unthinkingly convey to our

pupils in our attitude to black pupils, to 'other' cultural practices, to diversity? Here we see the need for a continuous process of professional development – of becoming aware of our own ethnocentric assumptions and prejudices and of the racism of the society and education system in which we work.

2. In the second section we considered our educational aims and objectives – what developments we should seek in our pupils and what changes the education system, and why these are worthwhile. Raising basic questions about our values and the justifications for what, as educators, we do, made it clear that education must be anti-racist and pluralist. A narrowly monocultural and ethnocentric curriculum was seen to be miseducation.

3. In considering the nature of multicultural education we saw that it can be racist or anti-racist. Racist multicultural education is tokenist and 'other' cultures are perceived through ethnocentric spectacles. It reinforces racial and cultural prejudices. Anti-racist multicultural education, on the other hand, is genuinely pluralist. Knowledge, values and skills are drawn from a variety of cultural traditions. These are directly experienced to enable genuine understanding of a variety of languages, religions, cuisines, art forms, and so on. These are selected in the light of educational developments in which all groups have had a voice.

4. In considering anti-racism we recognized that anti-racist education will be concerned to develop a non-ethnocentric pluralist curriculum, but will also involve more than this. Extra-curriculum aspects of education – the institutional racism within the structures of the education system itself – must be changed too. Anti-racist education placed particular emphasis on the need to combat this structural discrimination.

5. The need to both combat racism and to develop a culturally plural curriculum is referred to as anti-racist multicultural education.

6. We examined the Swann Report's notion of diversity within a common framework of values and saw that some values are shared (universal) and some are culturally distinct. These two aspects of cultural diversity should be recognized and incorporated within education for our multicultural society. Such genuine multicultural education also rests on the values of the pluralist ideal and will itself play a part in the further and on-going development of a

common framework of values for a more equal and harmonious multicultural society.

The Nature of Change

Educational theory, then, should provide guidance for practice, and theoretical considerations have established that it is desirable to develop anti-racist multicultural education, and that this will require *changes* in practice; in the curriculum and also in LEA and school policies and procedures. We wish to move from discriminatory structures and an ethnocentric curriculum to equal opportunities and an anti-racist pluralist curriculum.

It is necessary, therefore, to give some consideration to how such changes can be accomplished. How does change work? What factors facilitate and what hinder change in an educational context? We need to think about the nature of change and the strategies by which particular changes can be successfully made.

The educational system is diverse. Power and authority is distributed between various groups and individuals, including central and local government, governors, headteachers and teachers, parents and pupils. Change will therefore be complex, slow and piecemeal – operating at various interacting levels. Frameworks provided by central government and the LEA constrain but do not determine what schools will be like. Individual schools have considerable, but not complete freedom within these imposed structures and constraints, and within each school what goes on in its various classrooms will be considerably influenced by individual teachers. Anti-racist progress will therefore require changes at three levels; that of the individual teacher, the individual institution and at central/local government level. All three levels interact and are influenced by many and diverse pressures.

Much of this book is addressed to the individual teacher and how she can develop her own understanding and thus change her own classroom practice. By reflecting on previous changes which have taken place in her institution, she may also gain ideas about how to influence the school as a whole. What changes have been successfully implemented and what factors were significant in this change process? We will consider these questions here, and examine change at local authority level in the section on the LEA.

Of course some institutions are an easier challenge than others, but any institution will have strengths and weaknesses and features which yield relatively easily to change and others which are more entrenched. It is important to think about the character of the institution before embarking on changing it.

The next stage is to clarify the values underlying the wish for change, so that they can be seen in relation to the school's educative function. At this point one can work out specific goals and an action plan to achieve them. It is important to identify achievable goals. Where the action plan requires resources which are lacking (financial, administrative, human, and so on) the action plan should include realistic steps to achieve them.

Basically change will come about if the cost of the change, in both financial and psychological terms, is generally perceived to be less than the level of dissatisfaction with the present situation, within the institution, combined with a clear view of the desired goals and the practical steps required to achieve them. An individual or group of individuals develop a concern about the present situation in members of the institution until the need for change is generally acknowledged and understood. There is thus pressure for change at grass roots level. Ideally, combined with this, key people in the institution should then be involved in planning the action to be taken. A key aspect within the change process is that of leadership and management.

An individual teacher is most likely to influence her school or her LEA by working collectively with other like-minded individuals in pressure groups of various kinds. The process of change is important and the more people who are involved in that process the more effective the change is likely to be. Moreover, such democratically wide involvement is consonant with the values underpinning the wish for these particular kinds of change.

In effect we have identified three principles for the individual teacher who wishes to change her institution: (a) consider the nature of change and recent changes which have successfully occurred in your school; (b) recognise the importance of process and seek to initiate working groups/tasks; (c) network and collaborate with others. In addition, one can develop the more *ad hoc* habit of identifying and exploiting loopholes in situations as they arise.

Finally, one must recognize that however effective the change strategies, there are limits to what any individual can achieve. Moreover, and without going into ideological debates about which comes first, the egg of the individual psyche (liberal) or the chicken of the social order (marxist) there are limits on how much change in our eduction system is possible within our political and economic context; and limits too, on how far *educational* change could, in turn, change that context.

Nevertheless, as teachers we have a professional duty to provide the best education we can. How then should we develop a curriculum and practices within our own classroom which are appropriate to our multi-cultural society?

Positive and Negative Approaches

So far we have said that a negative approach to developing a multicultural curriculum will involve tokenism and ethnocentricity. It will be tokenistic if superficial, and ethnocentric if 'other cultures' are only apprehended through the spectacles of the dominant culture – that is in the light of majority assumptions, values and beliefs. Such approaches reinforce our tendency to regard the dominant culture as the norm from which others deviate.

For example, in a primary school, a class might 'do' a project on India. This will be negative if the project is unrelated to the rest of their curriculum (tokenistic) and if it encourages the idea that minority cultures are 'exotic' and -strange' (ethnocentric). In a secondary school a negative project approach will, for example, mean a whirlwind look at 'world faiths' (tokenistic) from a Christian perspective (ethnocentric).

A negative approach tends to be concerned only with lesson content and learning materials, leaving untouched the deeper 'procedural' level of the curriculum. In other words, there is no recognition that there may be diversity at the levels of conceptualizations and values. We saw, in Chapter 2, that there are shared universal values, forms of knowledge and principles or rational thought, *and* culturally distinct ones too. One negative approach will be to fail to convey that the universal features of human experience and knowledge *are* universal. They will be presented as in some way the special prerogative of the white Western world. A second negative approach will be to fail to include the culturally distinct aspects of human experience and knowledge – except for that which is distinctive of the dominant group.

Thus a negative approach at primary school would be to recognize only one family pattern – rather than to look at families across cultures; or, at secondary level, to recognize only one set of religious rituals (Christian) rather than to look at the use of ritual in a variety of religious traditions. In order to avoid such ethnocentricity, many teachers do take a theme approach to curriculum development; a theme approach which assumes that there are universal features in all families and in all uses of religious ritual.

Unfortunately, the culturally distinct features of family groupings or of religious traditions (except in the case of the dominant pattern) may be denigrated, or simply be omitted altogether. A non-tokenist curriculum pluralism would involve, for example, empathetic apprehension of the internal logic of Islam as well as Christianity.

While we maintain our relatively homogenous teaching force it is difficult to provide pluralism at this deeper level. For this reason the development of a culturally plural curriculum entails a more diverse teaching force, with an increased number of teachers from minority ethnic groups (see Chapter 6).

Having said what a negative approach to multicultural education comprises, we see, conversely, what a positive approach will be like. Pluralism will not be tokenistic but will permeate all parts, aspects and levels of the curriculum. In other words, it is not so much a case of adding in bits taken from 'minority cultures', here and there. Rather, there is a reorientation in perspective which influences teaching approaches, relationships with pupils, the teacher's values and assumptions and lesson content across the curriculum. It will not be ethnocentric but will involve recognizing universal knowledge, values and experience as universal, and initiation into culturally distinct ways of experience and forms of knowledge. This last will tend to require (think of language and religion) teachers working cooperatively and drawn from a variety of ethnic backgrounds.

Taking a specific example of curriculum development, let us see what all this amounts to in practice, in terms of what teachers should and should not do.

Table 4: Analysis of Negative and Positive Approaches

What to do and what not to do

Negative	Positive
1. Total omission	1. Permeation
2. Ethnocentricity	2. Pluralist perspective

Let us consider a popular primary school project – 'Heroes and Heroines'. To fail to include any heroes and heroines from minority ethnic groups would be to take an negative approach. Are all the people selected for study white Anglo Saxon men, or (less likely) white Anglo Saxon men and women or (even less likely) black and white men and women from a variety of ethnic backgrounds? Is one token black hero or heroine included – or 'representational' numbers? How are these figures selected and presented? The selection of black people who further or who represent some 'white' cause or value does not constitute pluralism.

A positive approach to the project would be designed to introduce the children to a range of significant individuals from various backgrounds. It would also encourage pupils to explore the notion of 'hero' and 'heroine' and consider what action and qualities *should* be valued and admired. Do the children understand that there is not just one possible answer here? And are they understanding the social, historical context from which this person did what she did? And have some neglected individuals and groups (women, black people, oppressed classes) been rescued form obscurity?

An example of such a 'rescue' is provided by a 'nursing' project which introduces Mary Secole – a relatively neglected heroine of the Crimean War. After she appeared in recently published books (Alexander and Dewjee, 1984) and posters she began to feature in some primary school work. How easy for her to become a token black in the kind of negative approaches I have described. The positive approach (part of a genuinely more anti-racist pluralistically permeated curriculum) would take the opportunity to raise the question, with the children, of why she *is* less well known than the comparable Florence Nightingale, and to explore the prejudice and discrimination she had to face and overcome, and her courage in so doing.

The Role of Parents and Governors

Good schools work with their pupils' parents – recognizing that the education of children requires a partnership between home and school. Some multi-ethnic schools have home/school liaison teachers, funded through Section 11. Multicultural education has encouraged parental involvement in schools, emphasized the importance of dialogue between parents and teachers and also of the need for consultation of parents about educational matters. Because schools have been failing their black pupils, the views of black parents about improving the situation will be very important.

Obviously language barriers should not be permitted to hinder either communication or consultation. Parents who do not speak English should be catered for – through translation of letters home and through the provision of interpreters on key occasions. Teachers and officers could also try to avoid bureaucratic language. In keeping with the democratic values previously emphasized, consultation should include some parental involvement in decision making so that black and white parents are genuinely part of education developments affecting their children.

Given the endemic racial prejudices of the white community, anti-racist education is an important task for adult educators and for all those concerned with parental education. Teachers, particularly in predominantly white areas, have found parental attitudes a problem, impeding the anti-racist multicultural education of the children.

With the Education Reform Act, an increased number of governors will be parent-governors. There is potential for an increase of parental influence and of more black parents on governing bodies. With ERA, too, governors are to have more power. They will be responsible for the school budget, for hiring and firing teachers and for curriculum related decisions. Currently more training for governors is being developed in recognition of these new responsibilities. Governors should take training opportunities which are offered to them, while those with responsibility for such training ought to ensure that the training incorporates anti-racist multicultural education.

The Local Education Authority and LEA Support Services

Equal opportunity policy statements could be made by central government. In some countries, but not his one, they have been. They have been made here by substantial numbers of local authorities. In some areas the equal opportunity policy on employment practices and service delivery relates to the local authority as a whole, including the education department. In others it is the LEA which has produced the policy, which thus relates specifically to the education service. There is also variety in the scope of the documents. For some authorities, ILEA for example, the documents cover race, sex and class. Others include just race and gender, yet others only race – in terms of multicultural education for some authorities and anti-racist education for the more progressive. Avon (where I used to be the Adviser for Multicultural Education) started with a multicultural policy, went on to an equal opportunity policy covering race, sex, disability and sexual orientation, but not class, and is currently replacing the multicultural policy with an anti-racist one.

There are also differences between authority statements in comprehensiveness. While some policies are general statements of principle and intent, others additionally provide guidance on procedures for its implementation.

Some schools and colleges have also developed equal opportunity policies – with a similar variety in scope, comprehensiveness and ideology. A number of LEAs have required such statements from their institutions.

Berkshire produced one of the earliest LEA policies. It was on racial equality and it influenced several other LEAs. It placed emphasis on racial justice – on equality of outcome, as well as on equality of opportunity. Thus it incorporated the notion that we need to concentrate not on the intention behind educational practices and procedures but on their outcomes. Non-discriminatory practices and procedures yield outcomes which are equitable and just.

The philosopher Antony Flew criticized Berkshire and ILEA on the grounds that there is no necessary connection between equality of opportunity and equality of outcome – that the absence of the latter does not entail the absence of the former. This is logically correct in a formal sense. There is no *logical* connection between inequality of outcome and inequality of opportunity. Nevertheless, as a matter of fact, inequality of outcome is usually a good indicator that there is indeed inequality of opportunity – that the situation requires scrutiny and change. There is substantial empirical evidence that inequality of opportunity is a significant factor in inequality of educational outcomes between girls and boys and between black children and white.

The Berkshire policy incorporates a general policy statement and papers on its practical implications and recommended support. (It is reproduced in the Swann Report (1985), Chapter 6, Annex A.)

It is interesting and sad that the Berkshire County Council sought, in 1988, to rescind this long established policy. Fortunately, such was the response from large numbers of individuals and organizations writing to ask them to reconsider and be proud of their influential documents that the policy has been saved – a useful pointer, perhaps, to the potential effectiveness of large scale collective pressure.

Various views have been expressed about both local authority and institutional policies: there are those who see them as having a *crucial* role in initiating a change process and others who see them as 'not worth the paper they are written on'. Certainly policy statements are not a panacea and are only worthwhile in so far as they are translated into non-discriminatory procedures and practices, which does not happen immediately. They do not suddenly re-orientate the educational practice in each classroom or end at one stroke all the discriminatory structures within the LEA. Nevertheless they do help to provide a climate conducive to such changes and can be a trigger for action. They can also be used to legitimate equal opportunity initiatives which some would seek to resist. They provide a support and an endorsement, a justification and a guide for anti-racist initiatives at all levels within the LEA. They are, therefore, to be worked for and welcomed.

In a paper entitled 'The Politics of Race in Britain' Ben Tovin *et al.* (1986) identified three factors influencing local authority development on equal opportunities: spontaneous protest, pressure for community resources and planned political struggle. All three factors are necessary for LEA level change, but may still be insufficient. The broader social and political conditions are also important. Ball has identified three further themes for understanding the formation and implementation of local authority equal opportunity policies – corporate provision, co-option and consultation. The complex internal organizational apparatus of local authorities calls for corporate strategies such as the establishment of special units with specific tasks. Co-option is a way of ensuring black and community participation in local authority decision making though in practice the co-optees are sometimes unrepresentative and in any case often denied full participation and voting rights. Similarly consultation often fails to give community groups a significant voice. However, it is clear that change at LEA level requires action within the local authority structures and external pressures and involvement. Moreover, a stronger voice for black people must be generated in the change process, and become built into any new structures and routine procedures which emerge.

A case study of Avon would, I believe, support the Ben Tovin and Ball analyses. Certainly the urban disturbances in Bristol in 1981 and subsequent Home Office enquiry were influential in the decision to establish a multicultural education policy. Sustained pressure by community groups for resources and sustained political struggle by groups such as teachers at Bristol's Multicultural Education Centre, the BCRE (Bristol Council for Racial Equality) and the Campaign for Anti-Racist Education pressured politicians on these matters. A local authority equal opportunities unit working directly under the Chief Executive was set up. This unit produced the generic policy to which I have referred. More recent urban disturbances and continued increased pressure led to the setting up of a black advisory group to advise the authority on an anti-racist education policy to replace the earlier multicultural statement.

These changes were made by the then labour controlled city council, on which there were a number of committed and influential members. The Multicultural Education Centre and Equal Opportunities Unit worked from within the local authority. Such internal pressure for more co-option and wider consultation strengthened the black voice in decision making and local authority accountability to local communities.

The process of consultations with local community groups, parents and schools generates discussion at various levels and puts multicultural education firmly on the local authority agenda. Thus the process of obtaining a policy is often more important in changing the climate of opinion than the product itself.

The Lea Support Services

Many local education authorities have a central multicultural support service. Often the staff who comprise these centres are funded through Section 11. This means that they are not funded to assist predominantly white institutions, but confine their promotion of multicultural education to the 'special needs' dimension. Moreover, many would argue (including the Swann Report) that meeting special needs such as E2L (English as a second language) should be a mainstream provision. Children should not be withdrawn to separate language centres or to special classes. Some centres do also have staff who undertake anti-racist work in white schools. It could be argued that agents for anti-racist change are more effective if they are members of a school staff, rather than such visiting 'specialists'.

Nevertheless, specialist teachers have often developed an expertise in a particular aspect of multicultural education: it might be in teaching English as a second language, or in knowledge of the work of black British writers, or in a particular world faith, and so on. And in fact many dedicated teachers work in multicultural support services and are highly motivated and competent in relation to promoting anti-racist education. Often a higher proportion of black and bilingual teachers work in such centres than in mainstream institutions. Thus, despite ideals about mainstreaming, and the permeation of anti-racist and pluralist perspectives, many schools and their pupils do benefit from specialist LEA multicultural provision.

The Role of the Adviser

About 60 local education authorities have one or more advisers for multicultural education. Advisers have a dual responsibility. They both advise the LEA (usually the Chief Adviser and the Director of Education) in matters relating to race, culture and education, and they also advise schools.

Sometimes the adviser contacts all schools within the LEA and sometimes s/he approaches a particular school. Often, however, a headteacher, teacher or school governor makes the contact – seeking advice about multicultural education. There are at least five ways in which your adviser for multicultural education may be able to be of use: with advice and relevant information; to provide support for your anti-racist multicultural initiatives; to create fruitful links and contacts; to suggest and facilitate appropriate in-service training; and, for some purposes, with (usually fairly limited) financial assistance.

The adviser will welcome your interest and enthusiasm for multicultural education and will wish to be of use. Moreover, in learning about what particular teachers and schools are doing, s/he increases her own knowledge about developments in the LEA. A word of caution, however; good advisers are busy people with limited time for any one initiative, individual or school.

Advice and Information

From wide experience in the field, the adviser will have helpful suggestions on any relevant matter about which you would welcome advice. Sometimes it is helpful just to talk through your idea or problem. And, through keeping up with national and local developments, the adviser should be a useful source of information about resources, good practice, national conferences and so on.

Support and Encouragement

We all work and feel better with encouragement and support. It may be particularly helpful for a teacher in a rather unsympathetic school to receive the direct support of the LEA adviser. Moreover, the adviser may be able to provide additional resources of staff or materials, for example from the LEA multicultural support service.

Links and Contacts

A teacher, or group of teachers, may be undertaking an initiative, similar or supplementary to others in that or other LEAs. Or it may be that their curriculum development could benefit from the experience or knowledge of some individual or organization outside of the school. By keeping informed of local and national initiatives, and by liaising with relevant organizations and individuals, the adviser will often be in a position to facilitate links which will prove to be extremely helpful to anti-racist multicultural school based developments. Contact the adviser if some additional assistance is required. (Just keeping her informed of your initiative may bring unlooked for, but helpful, contacts.)

In-Service Training

Resources for in-service training are finite. Nevertheless make your wish for further training known. Some applications will be successful – and the adviser will be in a stronger position to argue for more INSET resources by being able to demonstrate that existing resources are inadequate for current demands. Moreover the adviser will know what INSET possibilities exist, in the LEA and within that locality, and elsewhere.

Financial Assistance

The adviser may have funds to assist worthwhile developments in individual schools. S/he may have a curriculum development budget, or a resources allocation, and the like. Therefore, teachers who have anti-racist multicultural development plans which require more financial backing than their school can (or will) provide should approach the adviser to seek financial assistance.

The Politics of Change

In this chapter we have considered the relationship between theory and practice and set down the principles to be drawn from the theoretical discussion of previous chapters. We have also considered the nature of change – and the role of parents, governors, the LEA, support services and advisers – particularly as they affect individual teachers who are seeking anti-racist multicultural changes in their work.

At this point we should perhaps pause to consider the political implications of seeking equalitarian changes of these kinds. It is a common mistake to suppose that education can be non-political. Questions of value, of the distribution of power and of resources, of social privilege and disadvantage are inescapably part of educational decisions. Preserving the status quo is as political as changing it.

The relationship between education and the society in which it takes place is complex. How far does the education system influence or simply reflect the society of which it is a part? To what extent could education become non-racist in a racist society? I have assumed, in the preceding chapters, that education, in its organization and its curriculum could become at least less racist, and that such equalitarian change is worthwhile.

The analytic model of multicultural education (Table 2) includes the ideological perspectives outlined at the outset, in Chapter 1. These ideological perspectives represent an historical development in multicultural education, but they are also all still discernable in current practice and debate. Integrationism is conservative – seeking for the assimilation of minority groups without significant social change. Cultural pluralism is liberal – seeking freedom for cultural traditions to flourish in harmony and mutual respect. Anti-racism is radical – seeking more fundamental structural change for greater equality between ethnic groups.

The movement towards equal opportunities in education, of which anti-racist multicultural education forms a part, also exhibits these liberal and radical ideologies. The liberal approach is concerned with justice for individuals. It seeks to ensure that each person can compete without unfair barriers connected with gender to ethnicity, on an equal basis for desirable goods. Thus sexually and racially discriminatory procedures have to be changed. A radical approach is concerned with justice for disadvantaged groups. It seeks to ensure a fair distribution of goods so that black people and women are proportionately advantaged. The disadvantages accruing to these groups from past discrimination have to be redressed through positive action.

Both these approaches to equal opportunities are keyed into a version of social organization based on competition for social rewards – rather than on real *need*. For example, academic high fliers receive more opportunities for longer and recurrent post-school education than those with learning difficulties – who have the greater need for more educational time. Both approaches are based on ensuring that more women and black people are among advantaged groups, rather than on seeking to eliminate disadvantage *per se*. What about the most vulnerable in whatever group?

As educationalists we should do the best we can for all our pupils – seeking for imaginative improvements in moral education which will enable pupils to relate more humanely to each other and in political education, to encourage them, as adults, to work towards a society in which there is not just equality of opportunity, but equality of outcome; in terms of decent material conditions for everyone, and in terms of the fulfilment of other non-material needs – universal needs, and individual ones reflecting each person's unique range of abilities, disabilities and interests. Anti-racist multicultural education contributes to this ideal.

Assuming, then, that anti-racist multicultural changes in education are, *theoretically*, both possible and worthwhile, in part two we shall be more directly concerned with the *practical* aspects of these changes in schools.

Because continuity in a child's educational experience is important, teachers, whether primary or secondary, should read both chapters 4 and 5. Secondary teachers will find much of what is said about resources, white schools and record keeping in the primary sector equally relevant to them. Conversely, primary teachers will find the curriculum checklists helpful, in chapter 5.

PART III
PRACTICE

Chapter 4
The Primary School

Organization and Ethos

Ideally, as we have seen, an anti-racist multicultural dimension will permeate school life, including all aspects of the curriculum and also the ethos and organization of the school as a whole. The school's ethos derives from the predominant values which are embodied in the relationships between people within the school and with parents and visitors, the visual environment and learning resources, the curriculum and extra-curriculum activities and the procedural structures for dealing with decision making, discipline, appointments, classing and so on. Obviously the role of the headteacher is a crucial one. Her (or more usually his) approach to racial justice and cultural diversity will be an important influence on the school as a whole. Nevertheless, the attitudes and actions of teachers, ancillary staff and governors will also affect the overall ethos. The more people who take multicultural education seriously and who seek to reflect democratic and humane values within their school, the more nearly that school will attain the 'whole school' ideal.

To provide a focus and guide for a whole school approach, some schools have constructed a policy on anti-racist multicultural education. Such policy documents vary enormously in length, detail and emphasis and also, of course, in reflecting their particular situation. (Samples of two primary school policies are described in detail in *Education for a Multicultural Society: case studies in ILEA schools,* edited by M. Straker-Weld, 1984.)

Just as there are advantages to having an LEA policy, so there are similar advantages at school level. They provide encouragement, support, justification and guidance for worthwhile developments in the school. A further important advantage lies in the value of the process of constructing such a policy. It is important that all the staff of the school are involved, so that they will feel able to 'own' the policy and also because the process is itself a learning one. In a small primary school all the staff can form the working group which produces the document. In a large secondary school involvement will be through representation, consultation and opportunities, during the construction process, for discussion, comment and modification.

The implementation of the school policy will be an ongoing task – and procedures for the assessment of its effectiveness should also be constructed. For example, who assesses the overall visual environment of the school and are they taking account of the anti-racist multicultural dimension? Even today, in many white schools, nothing in the visual environment – the posters, artifacts, drawings, paintings, and notices indicates that black people (or cultural diversity) actually exist. This is a paradigm of indirect miseducation. And how is the curriculum to be assessed and developed, and the extra-curriculum dimensions – the assemblies and celebrations and the out of school activities?

The procedural or organizational features of the school are also pervasive and affect both the well-being of those in the school community and the quality of learning that takes place. Are the procedures for appointment unwittingly discriminatory; for example, 'word of mouth' recruitment may bypass groups that are not part of a particular network of contacts? Are discipline procedures just and humane; for example, are there agreed procedures for dealing with racial abuse? How are classes organized; for example, in a school with Muslim children is physical education organized to allow for separate provision for boys and girls? Within classes do some of the children's tasks involve collaborative learning activities? Is the school rigidly hierarchical or does it allow more open discussion and shared decision making? Is the liaison with parents such that they too have a voice in developments?

Of course an individual teacher in an unsympathetic school is in a difficult position, with limited influence and change potential. However, there are strategies for such isolated people. Firstly, even the isolated teacher has considerable control within her own classroom – her curriculum content and teaching strategies, classroom displays and learning resources, relationships with pupils and her implicit values and perspectives. She can also seek to influence her more sympathetic colleagues and suggest multicultural education for a school based INSET programme. She can invite useful allies (advisers, and so on, as visitors and speakers, and share good learning resources – for example in team teaching). She cannot do everything but she does what she can.

School and Classroom Resources

The school's learning materials must be anti-racist and culturally diverse in order to support multicultural curriculum developments. In many schools, particularly white schools, nothing in the visual display, books and other learning materials would suggest that black people actually exist! Where they are portrayed or mentioned, the images and assumptions are almost always negative (as they are in the media) portraying black people as inferior, strange, violent, stupid, or comic. Such images *do* influence the children's perceptions of various groups. This is particularly the case in primary schools, for the children have not yet developed critical faculties to withstand such constant implicit indoctrination. The work of David Milner (1983) has shown the adverse effect such influences have had on the attitudes of even very young pre-school children. From nursery school on, teachers need to ensure that the images, assumptions and values that their pupils are exposed to, in the materials they use and create, are much more positive than they are when no such effort is made. Books, posters, toys, artifacts, reading schemes and so on should include positive images and accurate information about all ethnic groups and show people from these groups in a wide range of roles and situations.

Unless some thought has been given to selection criteria, a school's learning stock will almost certainly be racially biased and ethnocentric through *omission* as well as through *commission*. That is to say, minority ethnic groups are often simply invisible. Think of all those reading schemes which portray white mother (cooking), white father (repairing), daughter (helping mother) and son (helping father) meeting white male doctors and postmen and white female nurses and shoppers. Of course to have individual books, posters or dolls which are white is fine. The problem occurs when all, or almost all, are so. The question is how to achieve a balanced stock and what to discard as too damagingly racist.

In keeping with what was said earlier about a whole school approach, ideally all the staff should work out the school's criteria for selecting and discarding books and materials. This is possible in primary schools. (At secondary level departmental discussion may be more fruitful.) Some schools devote an in-service day to such discussions. They often find criteria suggested in books about resources are a helpful starting point to discussion – though the point is to arrive at a checklist of their own. I have included a set of questions I devised and have used (Phillips-Bell *et al.*, 1983) but more comprehensive ones are also available (see Bibliographies page 107).

TO CHECK FOR BIAS THROUGH OMISSION

- Is the book written from the standpoint of a multicultural society? Does it recognize cultural diversity? Does the book value this diversity? Does it show 'other'religions, languages, lifestyles as valuable?

- Does the book show equal regard for and acceptance of different ethnic groups?

- Are minority ethnic group characters featured as part of everyday life in a pluralist society?

- Are there people in the story with whom black or brown children could identify? Are there strong characters which can act as role models?

- Are such characters portrayed in a positive manner? Do they show evidence of the ability to make decisions about their own lives?

In short, are ethnic and cultural minorities present in both the text and the illustrations? Are they presented in a matter-of-fact, accepting, integral and positive way.

TO CHECK FOR BIAS THROUGH COMMISSION

- Is there any evidence of tokenism or stereotyping in the text? Does it fail to present people from British minority groups and from other cultures overseas as individuals with every variety of human quality and attribute?

- Does language convey prejudice by use of perjorative words such as 'native', 'uncivilized', 'backward', or the use of linguistic stereotyping, for example, white = pure, black = evil?

- Do illustrations show evidence of tokenism, caricature or stereotyping, or do they correctly represent the ethnic group depicted?

- Are 'other cultures' judged against British or European norms? Does the book fail to present customs, lifestyles and traditions in a manner which explains their value, meaning and role in a particular culture? Are non-European cultures seen exclusively in terms of the exotic? Is the superiority of European cultures assumed and is it seen as the desirable norm for all people? Is a different level of achievement or intelligence assumed?

- Are historical events seen exclusively from a European viewpoint? Do non-European countries appear to have no history until 'discovered' by Europeans? Is the contact of Europeans with other peoples throughout history described as beneficial to the other country?

- Is poverty attributed to lack of Western technology and expertise? Is development aid portrayed as inspired exclusively by altruistic motives of European countries?

- Does the book reinforce, either by text or illustration, the image of a power structure in which white people have all the power and make all the decisions, with members of minority ethnic groups in subservient roles?

In short, does the book contain anything which is damaging to the self-esteem of black children, or to the developing racial attitudes of white children, or to the development of a multicultural society?

In my experience an exercise which people find interesting and enlightening is for the staff to:

1. Work out your criteria for judging a stock of books as a whole.

2. Work out your criteria for judging an individual book to be ethnocentric.

3. Work out your criteria for judging an individual book to be so damagingly racist as to be removed. (Perhaps to be used with older children during lessons about bias, stereotyping and racism.)

A selection of the school's commonly-used books should be analysed (The group could be subdivided and cover more materials.) People are often amazed at how badly their learning materials come out of such analysis. The awareness of layers and levels of bias is enhanced in the process. People are sometimes momentarily amused at the ludicrous

statements, illustrations and assumptions they uncover, but the serious-
ness of the situation, for the children, strikes home.

Visual Display

A good primary school provides a stimulating and colourful visual environment, making extensive use of the children's own work, information
posters (numbers, colours, letters), pictures which are aesthetically arrest-
ing and/or relevant to work or activities in progress in the school or in a
particular class, and artifacts, fabrics and objects of all kinds. This visual
environment should reflect, positively, our multicultural and multiracial
society.

Travel agents and local health authorities may provide good posters and
leaflets. Take care to scrutinize these in line with your criteria however.
The children already see too many pictures of white holiday makers
served by black waiters, and black patients being treated by white doctors. (Try some reversals for balance.) Government information and tour-
ist offices and High Commissions may also be helpful. Magazines, colour
supplements, postcards, minority newspapers, local education authority
multicultural education support centres and art loan services may be a
source of pictures and posters. The education journal of the Commission
for Racial Equality (address page 108) often contains useful photographs
of groups of black and white children.

Thematic and Project Displays

In the next section we shall consider culturally plural approaches to primary school project work. Some of the sources mentioned above will provide posters, pictures and leaflets that may be useful in this work. For
example, a project on 'People who work for us' should positively portray
occupational groups at all levels. The inclusion of photographs of a black
woman doctor and a white male nurse would help to contradict existing
stereotypes, while shops run by Indian, Pakistani and Caribbean traders
are a rich source of materials for many projects (for example, on fruits
and foods of various kinds).

Activity Materials

In nursery and primary education children use and handle a variety of
things: dolls, games, jigsaw puzzles, dressing up clothes, home-corner
utensils. More publishers and educational suppliers are including such

materials in their catalogues (see page 108). These are sometimes expensive but can be supplemented by free materials loaned by the LEA through its various support services. Parents, too, will often lend or give clothes and cooking utensils.

Reading Schemes

There is still discussion about how children best learn to read but most schools still use a structured reading scheme, albeit supplemented with more varied reading material. Many schemes omit pluralism and ethnic diversity and some are explicitly racist. Reading schemes, then, also need to be scrutinized according to the criteria which the staff (or at least you) have constructed. Some schemes have attempted a multicultural approach. As more publishers are adding to their materials, it can be useful to keep an eye on the 'multicultural' journals for suggestions and reviews, to find better reading schemes and other materials.

World Studies

Geography books contain some of the most blatant examples of ethnocentricity and racist generalizations. Fortunately more teachers are recognizing that education should have a global, internationalist perspective and there have been progressive developments in world study projects, including the School's Council sponsored (and published) *World Studies 8–13 Project (1985)*. These publications are informative and do not denigrate third world cultures. Unfortunately, many books about other countries adopt a patronizing attitude – a racist legacy of Britain's colonial past.

The Commonwealth Institute has educational facilities and has updated its galleries of artifacts and information on Commonwealth countries. The Institute will also provide speakers for classes who visit their premises, and even go out to schools in London and when staffing permits, to other areas. It holds exhibitions of art and literature, providing regular information booklets on these activities and services to schools. (Address page 108.)

Library and Classroom Books

Books are expensive and no doubt, much as one might wish it, few schools will have the opportunity to build up their book stock from scratch. Using your criteria, the most damagingly racist books should not be used, or at least not without comment, or as an aid to learning about racism. All future purchases should conform to the checklist of criteria or questions which the school has constructed. It is likely that a current imbalance will mean that most additional books will for some time be strongly pluralist in perspective or focused on, and written by members of, a minority culture. During this period of achieving a more balanced book stock, make use of the school's library loan service, explaining your objective.

Useful journals which review books and publish lists of titles can be found in the resources section.

These considerations apply to both fiction and non-fiction. Fiction provides the opportunity to read black authors writing about the experiences of black families and the adventures of black and white children Information books should be accurate and pluralist and internationalist in perspective. The illustrations and pictures in books are important, as well as the content. Implicit assumptions and values are important as well as what is overtly stated. Books about a minority ethnic group or some aspect of a minority culture (art, cruise, religion and so on) are usually best written by a member of that group. And surely schools which have children who speak (and read) languages other than English should have books in those languages.

It should be remembered that it is not just books and learning materials which constitute a learning resource. People are a resource too, including parents, visitors and (especially in multi-ethnic schools) the children themselves. Agencies of various kinds may also be useful as learning resources. I have already mentioned the CRE (Commission for Racial Equality). Multicultural Education Centres and the Commonwealth Institute. There may be reasonably accessible community or voluntary agencies involved in education, such as Oxfam and regional anti-racist organizations. Videos and television programmes can also be useful. Some audio-visual resources are listed in the resource section (page 110).

Some resources can be bought – from some mainstream publishers and from voluntary organizations (see resources section). Since multicultural education should permeate the curriculum, mainstream budgets should be spent within a pluralist perspective. In addition, special sources of funds may be available – for particular projects and so on. LEAs ought to include funding in their ERA formulae, both in relation to anti-racist multicultural education for all (in line with the Swann Report) and for the special needs of multi-ethnic schools.

Some resources can be obtained free, and it is worth remembering that resources can also be made – by the teacher and by the children themselves. Children will need guidance and support in this. They cannot, for example, create a street scene which includes a variety of people if the materials they use (say cut-out figures) do not allow for this. Similarly, for their own drawing and painting of people, the teacher should have discussed, matter of factly, the variety of skin tones and how to mix the paints for realistic results. The ACER video (Afro-Caribbean Education Research Project). 'To School Together', shows children in a multi-ethnic class drawing and describing themselves and each other. (See page 110.) They are developing skills of observation, measurement and communication. The teacher unselfconsciously helps the children to observe and reproduce the variety of skin tones and hair textures. It is an excellent example of primary stage skills being developed by a teacher with an unforced, low key and effective anti-racist awareness.

Resources on their own do not produce anti-racist multicultural learning. It is sometimes rightly said – 'better an unbiased teacher using biased resources' than vice versa. Nevertheless, resources have a contribution to make; as does the process by which a teacher (or school) identifies and acquires a stock of good learning materials.

Curriculum Matters

What and how young children learn matters. At this stage children have not fully developed their critical faculties and accept what is presented to them by the authoritative adults in their lives. This is true of the implicit values, assumptions and behaviour of those adults, as well as what they explicitly say. Much of what children learn is 'caught not taught'.

In many primary schools children spend much of each week for one school year with 'their' teacher. Therefore, the teacher's attitude and approach is crucial. Obviously any one teacher has limited knowledge. What matters is adopting an anti-racist pluralist perspective to re-orientate the curriculum – not to change its content *per se*. The ACER video previously mentioned shows teachers using ACER learning materials with just such an approach. The usual primary school activities (drawing, reading, writing, calculating) and their associated skills (observation, categorization, and so on) are permeated, matters of factly, with an anti-racist, pluralist awareness. The teaching does not elevate one dominant 'norm' or standard or language: as one child puts it – 'In different places, people have a different *proper*'. Good teachers bring in other teachers – including the children themselves.

Many teachers have developed an interest in PSE (Personal and Social Education). Since personal education involves developing each child's self-esteem and confidence; and social education their empathy and respect for others, such PSE must involve anti-racist pluralist perspectives.

In a school where little multicultural work has been done, children may show some initial embarrassment. Several teachers have discussed this with me: particularly those in predominantly white schools, whose small number of minority ethnic group children have reacted this way. The phenomenon is also described by the Schools Council Working Party on Multicultural Education. In an ethnocentric school, where home and school are alien, there will be unease when these alien worlds come together. What a sad reflection on the school! We see here, again, the need for a whole school approach. Even without this, the class teacher's own matter of fact interest in cultural diversity will soon be 'caught' by her pupils. This should be combined with sensitivity to individual pupils.

Two general curriculum principles emerged from Chapter 2.

1.   Cultural traditions embody universal features, and also have distinctive features of their own. These are valid; not deviations from a 'norm' established by the dominant ethnic group.

2.   The curriculum should have an anti-racist as well as a pluralist dimension. In other words, in addition to countering cultural racism, it should counter negative racial stereotypes and address issues of prejudice and discrimination (as we saw earlier in the Mary Secole example).

These principles should be incorporated into primary school project work. Universal features associated with each project can be looked at across cultures, and distinctive features incorporated too.

Alison Sealey (1983) has contrasted ethnocentric and pluralist approaches to project work. She also points out that in a multicultural school a project on 'ourselves' or 'our community' *must* be culturally plural. The theme can be subdivided into a number of topics which can readily bring in a pluralist dimension in white schools too: including homes, food, worship, communication, facilities and clothes. The universal features are readily apparent. For example, we all need food for survival, and a balanced diet for health. The distinctive cultural cuisines all exhibit the principles of nutrition; variety of dishes, savory and sweet; cookery skills; and special dishes associated with special occasions such as religious festivals, weddings and so on. Suggestions of ways of linking food with various areas of the curriculum, and a related reading list are provided in 'Food as a resource for learning in the primary school', ILEA 1979. In exploring cross cultural universals, the more distinctive cultural features simultaneously and naturally emerge. Associated story reading can also be taken from several cultural traditions, for example *Share-a-story*, ILEA 1979 and *Folk Tales for Reading and Telling*, (BERG, 1976). Mary Smith (retired teacher from Avon's Multicultural Education Centre) has prepared a sample topic chart for two common primary school projects ('Homes' and 'The Recent Past') to suggest materials for an Afro-Caribbean input in such work. This can be found at the end of this chapter.

In my opinion the early years of education are often undervalued. Primary education lays the foundation for later learning. This foundation must include an anti-racist pluralist perspective which can be further developed at the secondary stage.

The Predominantly White School

The schools which, in my experience, have made most progress with a whole school approach to multicultural education tend to be inner city multiracial primary schools. Primary, being smaller than secondary schools, often forge more of a team approach. The staff know each other, all the pupils and their parents. Primary schools also tend to be more child centred in their teaching, and are therefore less likely to ignore their pupils' own experiences and home backgrounds. In the multiracial school, too, anti-racist multicultural issues are more readily perceived as relevant. Thus many 'multiracial' primary schools have developed a culturally plural dimension to their curriculum. (The children themselves, and their parents, are an invaluable learning resource.) They use 'minority' languages, have good home/school links, provide appropriate school dinners, celebrate a variety of religious festivals and so on. It is in the predominantly white schools that progress is at once more important in some ways, and more difficult.

It is more important in these white areas in the sense that racial prejudices, stereotyping and myths are particularly entrenched in areas where white people do not mix daily with black people and know them as friends. Studies have established that from an early age white children are developing these negative attitudes? (Milner, 1985). Moreover, it is in the more affluent of these white areas, in state schools in prosperous middles class locations and the independent sector, that those children are educated who will on the whole gain the most influential social positions. Do we want future politicians, industrialists, judges and chief officers to be racist, ethnocentric and narrow in their sympathies and experiences and thus to perpetuate current inequalities and injustice? Or do we educate to produce the kind of understanding and moral commitments which might help them to counter their own narrow self and group interest? In any case we owe it to these children not to miseducate.

Yet it is not easy to convince teachers, governors and parents in white areas that multicultural education is important. Many see it as relevant only to the inner city schools. 'We don't have that problem here' is frequently said. Significantly 'the problem' is equated with the presence of black people. We are unable to see that the real problem lies in our own prejudiced assumptions. For more advice on developing multicultural education in white areas see Chris Gaine's appropriately titled *No Problem Here* (1987).

There are obviously limits on the changes which an individual teacher can achieve in this kind of indifferent (or hostile) context. Nevertheless she can adopt some strategies to promote anti-racist, multicultural education in and beyond her own classroom. She can, perhaps through the adviser, make contact with other local like-minded teachers and governors for encouragement and support; invite useful visiting speakers on opportune occasions, (for example a black artist as part of a curriculum project, a sympathetic HMI or local adviser to talk about ERA (Education Reform Act)); show interesting learning materials to colleagues and seek contact between her school and a school similar in size and location, where anti-racist multicultural progress *has* been made.

Tests and Record Keeping

It is important to be aware that tests and record-keeping procedures may be culturally biased and to seek to eliminate such bias as far as one can.

One important dimension of bias relates to competence in Standard English. Where general intellectual, conceptual progress is being tested or recorded this should not be confused with competence in Standard English. Many general tests are unfair to children who are learning English as a second language or Standard English as a second dialect. The vocabulary and sentence structures may present an unnecessary and discriminatory obstacle. Very often, too, there is no recognition of the child's full language abilities – her bilingualism for example. And where competence in Standard English is what is at issue, testing and record keeping should be appropriate for an E2L pupil. In Avon for some years primary schools have kept a literacy record card for each child. This is passed on when the child moves to her secondary school. A working group of teachers subsequently developed a supplementary record card to ensure fairer record keeping for children whose first language is not English. It enables teachers to record home languages, progress in home languages, and conceptual development, as well as progress in learning English as a second language.

Range of cultural experiences and knowledge is a second dimension of bias. The questions, problems to be solved and examples provided should not be biased against any cultural group but should be appropriate for children from a wide range of backgrounds. Some children may have no experience of seaside holidays or Christmas celebrations, for instance. It is as easy to set an essay title appropriate to any celebration as to specify a Christian festival. A child's vocabulary is also, obviously, related to the range of experiences they have had. Much of what we learn is based on cultural conventions. Some of these we, the teachers, learned so long ago that we almost forget that they are not simply 'obvious'; that some children may have acquired culturally different approaches and understandings. For example, we do not simply understand cartoons and line drawings – we interpret them according to conventions we have earlier acquired. Because we take so much of what we learned as children for granted – as the natural way to act or understand, it is not always easy to notice this more subtle cultural bias. In multicultural schools it may be advisable to check for such bias in tests and record keeping procedures by consulting with a number of other adults with the relevant cultural backgrounds.

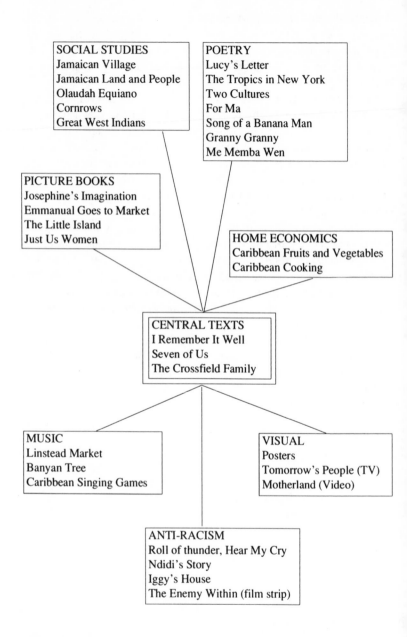

Figure 4.1: Topic Chart for Afro-Caribbean input to primary school projects

Bibliography for Topic Chart

Social Studies

HUBLEY, J. and HUBLEY, P. *Jamaican Village*, London:
    A & C Black.
FOLDER. X., *Jamaica Land and People*, Oxford: Oxfam.
KILLINGAY, D., *Olaudah Equiano and The Slave Trade*,
    Amersham, Bucks: Hulton.
YARBROUGH, C., *Great West Indians*, Longman Caribbean.

Poetry

BERRY, J., 'Lucy's Letter' from *Lucy's Letters and Loving*, BERRY,
    J., London: New Beacon Books.
McKAY, C., 'The Tropics in New York'. From *Caribbean Voices*, Vol
    1. London: Evans.
'Two Cultures' and 'For Ma', David Dabydeen. From: DABYDEEN,
    D., *Slave Song*, Dangaroo Press.
'Song of a Banana Man', JONES, E., from *Caribbean Voices*, Vol 1.
    London: Evans.
'Granny, Granny', NICHOLS, G. and 'Me Memba Wen',
    WILLIAMS, F. From: Ed. STYLES, M., *Like That Studd*,
    Cambridge.

Home Economics

WOOD, B. *Caribbean Fruits and Vegetables*. Longman Caribbean.
ORTIZ, E., *The Best of Caribbean Cooking*. London: Andre Deutsch.

Anti-racism

TAYLOR, M., *Roll of Thunder, Hear My Cry*. Puffin.
BABATUNDE, *Ndidi's Story*. London: A & C Black.
BLUME, J., *Iggy's House*
The Enemy Within. Filmstrip and book, London: British Council of
Churches.

Music

LEWIN, O. 'Alle, Alle, Alle'. Oxford: Oxford University Press.
LEWIN, O. 'Beeny Bud'. Oxford: Oxford University Press.
LEWIN, O. 'Brown Girl'. Oxford: Oxford University Press.
LEWIN, O. 'Dandy Shandy'. Oxford: Oxford University Press.
FROST, P. *West Indian Songs and Games. Bishop Road*, Bristol:
   Multicultural Education Centre.

Picture Books

DOBRIN, A. *Josephine's Imagination*. Leamington Spa: Scholastic.
CRAIG, K. *Emanuel Goes to Market*. Oxford: Oxford University Press.
LESSAC, F. *The Little Island*. Macmillan Caribbean.
CAINES, J. *Just Us Women*. London: Harper and Row.

Chapter 5
The Secondary School

Organization and Ethos

Much of what was said in the previous chapter about multiracial and also predominantly white primary schools and about resources can be readily transferred to the secondary sector. The question of school organization and ethos, however, is a different matter. Comprehensive secondary schools are, on the whole, much bigger than their neighbouring primaries. They tend to be more subject centred and so organized into curricular based departments.

Whereas in a primary school the class teacher is responsible for delivering the curriculum and also for her pupil's pastoral care, in secondary school the pupils learn from a range of teachers within the various departments and may have a pastoral tutor other than their form/class teacher.

This department structure gives rise to a number of implications for the development of anti-racist multicultural education.

1. Each department needs to develop an anti-racist multicultural perspective to their part of the curriculum. This will call for training, discussion and decisions within each department – with members collectively working out their anti-racist approach to teaching, resources, curriculum development and discipline. Clearly the Head of Department will have a key role in terms of encouraging the necessary changes.

2. For cross-curricular initiatives there will also need to be inter-departmental co-operation. For example, teachers from a number of departments might co-operate in teaching about racism within the Personal and Social Education programme. Similarly, teachers of subjects with strong links will need to know about each other's work.

3. Teachers responsible for English Language support of pupils for whom English is a second language, or standard English a second dialect, will ideally work alongside teachers of other subjects, rather than withdraw pupils from these classes. In either case, however, an E2L teacher (English as a second language) will need to know about her pupils' learning across the curriculum.

4. In addition to all this departmental level work, for the overall ethos of the school to be anti-racist and pluralist there must also be a whole school policy and an integrated approach. The headteacher is perhaps the biggest *single* influence on a school, with overall responsibility for management, including the tasks listed in Figure 5.1.

Clearly all these tasks have a multicultural dimension. It can be a worthwhile exercise for a group of teachers to formulate an anti-racist checklist to correlate with each of the education task areas to be managed.

Earlier we talked about developing a school policy on anti-racist multicultural education and the importance of the process involved and of democratic structures. A comprehensive policy will cover all the various aspects of school life, including those listed in the Managerial chart: philosophy, aims and objectives, consultation, decision making, administration, curriculum implementation, development and evaluation, teaching and learning methods, staff appointments, testing, record keeping, discipline, special needs, learning resources, external relations and school assessment. (A sample secondary school policy statement is described in detail in *Education for a Multicultural Society: Case Studies in ILEA Schools* (edited by M. Straker-Weld, 1984).)

It is important that the headteacher involves colleagues, and where appropriate, pupils and parents, not just in formulating the school policy, but in subsequent decisions and developments. This can be done even in large schools. For example the headteacher should discuss with staff what issues ought to involve parental consultation and how, where and when such consultation should take place. As many parents as possible should be involved and parental views then genuinely reflected in decisions. The language of consultation must not hinder communication. Therefore, languages of different communities may need to be used in the process. The school should also seek to avoid bureaucratic language, acronyms which may not be familiar and 'technical' education terms. A democratic approach ensures that everyone connected with the school can feel part of a just community.

Figure 5.1: Managerial Task Areas (with examples)

1. *Managing the Overall Policy:*
   philosophy, aims and objectives of school; long term plans; school leadership/management style; standards; management of time; school and the law; management of change; creation of atmosphere.

2. *Managing the school Communication and Decision Making Structures:*
   methods of consultation; provision of information; communication between staff; use and resolution of conflict; handling meetings; decision making; problem solving; team work; administration (forms), Staff Handbook.

3. *Managing the Curriculum (learning):*
   devising a curriculum policy; curriculum implementation, development and evaluation; teaching and learning methods; subject areas; timetabling; external examinations; homework policy; cover arrangements.

4. *Managing Staff:*
   maintaining effective relationships with teaching and non-teaching staff of both sexes; staff appointments; job descriptions; pastoral care of staff; motivation; staff development needs, reviews and provision; counselling and advice; delegation; role of staff with responsibilities; in-service training; teacher loads; probationers; student teachers; coping with stress; falling rolls; temporary dislocation.

5. *Managing Pupils:*
   arrangements for grouping, testing and assessment; pastoral care; record keeping; reports; discipline; regulations; continuity of education; special needs; social and personal development of all.

6. *Managing Material Resources:*
   buildings, equipment, furniture, materials; finance, capitation allocation; assessing needs; health and safety.

7. *Managing External Relations:*
   working with governors, LEA; relating to parents and wider school community; involvement of parents and governors in school; inter-school liaison; links with commerce and industry; media; support services.

8. *Managing the process of Monitoring and Evaluating the school:*
   assessment of all aspects of school life and its effect on pupils.

(Reproduced with permission from the National Development Centre, University of Bristol.)

The management task list also reminds us that the staff of a school includes non-teaching staff. Good anti-racist multicultural school based in-service training will include all staff, as will non-discriminatory recruitment and interview procedures and non-discriminatory delegation and promotion policies.

What was said in the previous chapter about the testing and assessment of pupils also applies at the secondary stage. In the following section we will consider other aspects of the pastoral care of pupils, including discipline, and the transition from school to work. The remaining parts of the chapter will focus on curriculum issues.

Pastoral Care

Children move from a small or relatively small primary school to a larger secondary comprehensive, in a bigger building, with a bewildering range of 'new' subjects and teachers. In their years of secondary education they will experience the changes and pressures of adolescence. Good secondary schools, therefore, recognize the need for a system of pastoral care as a key component in the organization and management of the institution. Ensuring each pupil's individual well-being is both humane and a necessary condition for fully effective educational progress. Whatever the system, pastoral care should find expression in curriculum terms through the personal and social development of pupils, in counselling as necessary, in good home/school liaison, in discipline practices and in careers guidance. All of these have an anti-racist multicultural dimension.

Many schools now explicitly recognize the importance of PSE (personal and social education); of a person-centred approach. We educate not minds, but persons, in all their holistic complexity – mental, moral, social, behavioural, emotional, spiritual, sexual. This emphasis on persons, as developing selves in relationship with other selves is, like multicultural education, not an additional bit on the curriculum but a reorientation of it all. And like multicultural education, its aims are fundamental – involving explicit thinking about what kind of society and what kinds of persons we are seeking to develop. Both PSE and multicultural education recognize the importance not just of the content of the curriculum but of the learning process, of implicit values and assumptions, and the relationship between teacher and learner. And they actually overlap in a concern for curriculum development which will counter racial prejudices as pupils develop, and which will equip them with anti-racist skills. (Do black pupils, for example, learn about what redress may be open to them in cases of racial discrimination?)

Research has shown that a person centred approach, in which the teacher has a positive relationship with and expectation of all pupils has significant educational benefits. Patrick Whitaker (Whitaker, 1988) reports on research by Carl Rogers which involves study of 3700 hours of classroom activity from 550 schools. Three particular kinds of teacher behaviour turned out to be especially significant:

1. The teacher's ability to understand the meaning that classroom experience is having for each pupil.

2. The respect and positive regard the teacher has for each pupil as a separate person.

3. The ability of the teacher to engage in a genuine person-to-person relationship with each pupil.

It was found that pupils in classes with teachers who demonstrated these qualities to a high degree made significantly greater gains in learning. They

*   became more adept at using higher cognitive processes such as problem solving;

*   had a higher self-concept;

*   exercised greater learning initiatives in the classroom;

*   exhibited fewer discipline problems;

*   had a lower absence rate.

What is particularly interesting and important is the conclusion that with specific training teachers can begin to change their attitudes and develop the sort of facilitative styles described above. The other main characteristics of such teachers were that they:

*   had a more positive self-concept than lower level teachers;

- were more open and self-disclosing to pupils;

- responded more often and more positively to pupils' feelings;

- gave more praise and encouragement;

- were more responsive to pupils' own ideas;

- engaged in formal didactic teaching less often.

However, let us look more specifically at some of the practical issues of pastoral care in a multicultural society.

Many teachers have not received training in counselling skills, and many have not developed an awareness of their personal prejudices, and how these may influence their perceptions of, and relationships with, black pupils. This indicates the need for appropriate INSET for white 'pastoral care staff' and the desperate need for more black teachers. There will be issues and problems connected with racial discrimination which black pupils may find easier to discuss with teachers who they know will have faced similar experiences in their own lives.

Some schools have home/school liaison teachers. Their aim should be more than to do 'case work' with pupils in difficulties. They need time, too, to help the school to develop good home links, to set up opportunities to encourage parents into school and to ensure the development of good practice, for example in the use of appropriate community language for letters sent to parents/guardians at home.

In developing discipline procedures the elimination of scope for racial bias should be a consideration. Agreed procedures, universally applicable, help to ensure that black pupils are not treated less favourably than white. Many teachers are still working with stereotyped expectations – and children (adult too!) often behave as others expect. In some cases there may be instances of 'cross cultural' misunderstanding. For example, many Afro-Caribbean children have learned, at home, that it is rude to look directly at an adult who is reprimanding you, and may appear to the teacher to be insolently refusing to 'look at me when I talk to you'.

Another important discipline issue concerns racial incidents – racist graffiti, racist abuse and so on. These should never be ignored by the school. In a primary school, very young children using racial abuse require an educative rather than a punitive response; but in secondary schools such racism should be recognized as a disciplinary matter. Teachers and support staff should know that racial abuse is not acceptable and should never be ignored. Procedures for dealing with such incidents should be developed. These procedures need to cover a range of situations. In more serious cases parents of the abuser and the abused should be informed.

Racial abuse is never justified. Even where a pupil resorting to such abuse was reacting to provocation, racism is not an acceptable form of response. Conversely, a black child reacting to racial abuse may react inappropriately (for example with physical violence). This may also require reprimand, but the teacher should understand the degree of provocation occasioned by racist taunts, and, in any case, should not overlook, and should be seen not to overlook, the original offence (the abuse).

Some LEAs have produced guidelines for their schools about dealing with racist incidents. Obviously these should be known by all staff.

Careers guidance is the last (but by no means the least) of the 'pastoral' dimensions previously mentioned. Whether such guidance involves merely giving vocational information and advice or seeks to assist and enable pupils to make informed and wise career decisions it is crucial that pupils should not be let down. Yet, as Elaine Foster points out:

> The observation and experiences of many black Afro-Caribbean parents and pupils of careers teachers and officers strongly suggest that very few teachers have been prepared to care for and vocationally guide black pupils. Only a small number have actually addressed themselves to the task of getting rid of the 'common-sense' prejudices of personal racism which have often dictated their interaction with black pupils. This is evident in the way some teachers have perpetuated the idea that some black pupils have different and 'racially' innate abilities and predilections and are therefore suited for certain types of jobs or careers. So Afro-Caribbean girls are directed to nursing, Asian boys to a career in small businesses or the sciences, and Asian girls to domesticity, with the excuse that they are going to be married off anyway. Not only were these teachers stereotyping pupils but they were, and still are, paralysing and containing black pupils within parameters which are both unjust and debilitating. (Foster, 1988.)

The placement of black pupils for community and industrial prevocational experience may also expose them to racism. Foster suggests that agencies should be made aware of and asked to support the school's policies and that pupil's too should be enabled to challenge any discriminatory practices they encounter.

Sadly, as we know from the Eggleston report (1987) black youngsters have high expectations of further and higher education but are getting least from it. In terms of academic qualification, employment training and employment black pupils are disadvantaged through discriminatory practices and prejudiced assumptions. Watts and Law (1988) offer five strategies for careers teachers to consider in order to adequately meet the needs of their black pupils.

1.   To provide 'compensatory' teaching for ethnic minority pupils in employability skills and/or knowledge of the labour market.

2.   To extend the range of 'role models' to which ethnic minority youngsters have access.

3.   To extend the range of informal networks to which ethnic minority youngsters have access.

4.   To prepare ethnic minority pupils to deal with the racial discrimination they may meet in the labour market (and elsewhere).

5.   To explore socio-political issues related to the opportunities open to ethnic minorities.

Curriculum Approaches

It has been said several times that an anti-racist multicultural dimension should permeate the curriculum. But what does this mean exactly, and how, in a departmentalized secondary school, can it be done. Jon Nixon has put it this way:

> An alternative to accretion can be found in a strategy that is often referred to as 'permeation'. Here curriculum development in the field of multicultural education is seen, not in terms of additions to an existing structure, but in terms of rethinking and restructuring every aspect of the curriculum. Issues relating to multicultural education, in other words, are allowed to soak into the very fibre of schooling. (Nixon, 1985.)

Permeation, then, is not about bolting bits onto the curriculum but a pervasive interweaving of a pluralist perspective. Nixon suggests that such a development proceeds in three necessary but overlapping phases of development. First there will be small-scale innovations. These are likely to be subject centred and team based. It involves process as well as content, for, as Nixon points out, it involves a research stance by both teachers and pupils. It relies upon the discovery of new facts and new perspectives. The headteacher must ensure that departmental initiatives are discussed and understood by the staff as a whole. The second phase involves coordination and development of these small scale innovations within the broad curriculum framework of the school and the generation of a school policy. Nixon suggests a working party which will be composed of staff drawn from the various ranks of the management structure – such as head of department, probationary teacher and head of year. The working group will need a broad curriculum perspective incorporating considerations about content and organization of the curriculum, teaching styles and methods, attitudes and expectations of teachers and pupil selection and grouping. Phase three is consultation and evaluation of the school policy that emerged. These consultations and evaluations in turn generate further and improved small-scale innovations. Thus permeation becomes a cyclical process.

We can see various ways in which permeation contrasts with tokenism. Permeation involves all aspects and parts of the curriculum and not just sample bits of content here and there. In addition to the aspects mentioned by Nixon, we have also earlier noted the importance of shared democratic, anti-racist values within the pluralist perspective – together with an opportunity for pupils to understand a plurality of ways of life and forms of thought.

As an anti-racist pluralist perspective permeates curriculum departments through curriculum developments which are coordinated into an overall policy for the school, so overall aspects of school life are affected. It is important, for example, that the school library as well as individual department stock rooms provides an appropriate stock of books. It is important that the general ethos, visual environment and interpersonal relationships in corridors, playing fields and dining rooms matches the classroom developments.

It is to be hoped that the five ERA (Education Reform Act) subject working groups which are still deliberating follow the example of the Science rather than of the Maths groups. (See page 12.) In any event, there are several useful resources for subject centred curriculum developments. (See Resources list page 107.) The following section contains brief sample checklists to indicate the kinds of questions that can usefully be raised. (They are, of course, far from comprehensive.)

Curriculum Checklists

One way of assessing your own work or your school as a whole is by using a checklist of searching questions. The checklist you use might be one of a number which have been published; for example ILEA's *Aide Memoire For The Inspectorate*, or *Agenda For Multicultural Teaching* by Alma Craft and Gillian Klein (SCDC Publications, 1986). (See Bibliography page 104). Even better would be to look at a number of these and then construct your own. Best of all, of course, would be for a number of colleagues, representing different departments to draw up a school checklist, and for the members of individual departments to add their own subject based questions.

A school checklist might include:

SCHOOL POLICY

Does the school, for example:

- have a written policy statement on anti-racist multicultural education?

- have strategies for establishing good policies and practices?

- involve ancillary staff, parents and the wider community in its policy development?

- produce relevant statements and guidelines?

- have a policy on dealing with racial abuse and graffiti?

What support is given to teachers and pupils in developing strategies to combat racial prejudice and discrimination?

ETHOS AND ATMOSPHERE

for example:

- Has the school recognized and made accommodation for pupils' particular religious practices, diets and dress requirements – without isolating them from activities shared with other pupils?

- Are languages other than English, which are spoken by pupils in the school, used in displays and notices?

- Do the images projected in the school's displays (particularly in rural schools) – in halls, corridors and classrooms, reflect positively and relate in an appropriate way to the cultural diversity of:

  – wider British society?
  – the world?

PARENTS AND LIAISON

For example:

- Has the school developed means for liaising and collaborating successfully with parents over the education of all the children?

- Does the school actively seek the views and perceptions of parents about their children? Are these taken into account in the school's provision for each child?

- What particular provision is made to communicate with parents whose mother tongue is not English?

- Does the school take an initiative in developing useful links with local organizations which represent the interests of a range of ethnic and cultural groups?

Other whole school aspects might include: equality of opportunity, racial prejudice and discrimination, language policy, pastoral care, careers guidance, staff development and school resources.

Individual departmental checklists might include teaching strategies, resources, assessment and record keeping, relationships with pupils, liaison with parents, continuity and progression of learning as well as more subject specific questions. The latter will, of course, be different for each department and even for different subject within the department. Below are listed sample questions relating to modern languages. (This is, of course, merely an example, and not meant to be a definitive or comprehensive list.)

1. Does the school have a language policy?

2. Does the school promote a linguistic awareness that respects and values all forms of language?

3. Has progress been made in responding to the issue of linguistic diversity through the language policy and practice of the whole school?

4. Are staff knowledgeable about the home languages which their pupils speak, and do they see these as a potential or real strength in the school?

5. Does the school acknowledge and support pupils' bilingualism and promote an interest in their language amongst all pupils?

6. Are Asian languages used by the school – both in terms of teaching through the pupils' home languages and in the teaching of community languages as modern languages?

7. Is there timetable provision and examination entries for languages extending beyond the commonly taught European languages?

8. Is the school aware of the interrelationship of language teaching and religious instruction in some minority ethnic communities?

Combating Racism Across the Curriculum

We have an ideal of a whole school approach to multicultural education and of a curriculum which is permeated with this perspective. Yet in many secondary schools there is considerable variation between departments in their awareness, and their development of, an anti-racist multicultural curriculum. Recognition of this has led to various initiatives which seek to coordinate and encourage curriculum development in the school as a whole

In this section I want to describe, briefly, one such cross-curriculum approach.

In 1985/6 teachers from Avon's Multicultural Education Centre and Resources for Learning Development Unit collaborated to develop and facilitate a cross-curriculum course for secondary school teachers. The idea was that the schools involved should send three teachers – from their English, Humanities and Science departments. In this way it was hoped that there would be development across the curriculum.

The course included a racism awareness foundation – beginning with a study of:

- The Concept of Race;

- Racism in its Historical and Contemporary Context;

- Racism in Education;

- The School Response.

At this stage there were seminars led by the three subject groupings. The Humanities group produced some tentatively agreed principles. The Science group felt unready to produce an anti-racist science model but felt they were beginning to understand the pervasive nature of racism. The Multicultural Education Centre provided additional input on English and a chart outlining the issues involved was produced.

The course also involved action back in the school and feedback evaluation to the organizers.

There are other ways, in addition to INSET courses, in which cross-curriculum collaboration might be encouraged in secondary school. For example, cross-curriculum projects centred on an interdisciplinary theme such as 'The Environment'. It facilitates the permeation of an anti-racist multicultural perspective in the curriculum as a whole and enables teachers to learn across subject boundaries, from each other. With such developments across several departments it also becomes much more likely that extra-curriculum aspects of secondary school life will also progress.

Figure 5.2: Anti-Racist Principles in Humanities

1. Organization

1. Mixed ability pupil grouping should always be the aim.
2. Teachers should employ a wide range of learning strategies.
   Group work is likely to be particularly fruitful, but will need INSET support. Groups could devise their own learning agendas.
3. Teachers should see themselves as facilitators - allowing pupils space to work out their own ideas.
4. An 'integrated humanities' approach has more potential than separate subjects. Not only does it give control over content, something normally determined by the subject traditions rather than contemporary relevance, but encourages teachers to work together across subject boundaries.
5. Teachers should have agreed anti-racist checklists for selecting materials and reviewing current practice.

2. Perspective

6. All courses should have an international perspective.
7. All courses should emphasize links and interdependence between groups.
8. All courses should give due consideration to the historical background to contemporary issues.
9. All courses should develop pupil's critical consciousness.
10. Humanities courses have a particular responsibility for dealing with value laden issues. Teachers will need INSET assistance to do this well.
11. Schools should seek a black perspective on the overall coverage of their humanities curriculum.
12. Courses should emphasize common features of human societies.

3. Content

13. All courses should include the black perspective within the curriculum, where posible using authentic voices.
14. Racism should be dealt with in an explicit way at clearly identifiable points throughout the humanities curriculum. This would be supplemented by an anti-racist perspective throughout.
15. Humanities has a particular responsibility for giving black pupils the opportunity to talk together about the reality of racism as they experience it.

(Avon Multicultural Education Centre)

Figure 5.3: English in Whole School and Society Context

Communication

Literature

part of accepted
canon, expectations
of exam system —
challenging the
canon, re-reading
texts, introducing
black authors –
criteria for selection,
effect of coursework

Language

conflict between use
of standard English,
questioning of appro-
priateness value of
diversity – how to
reconcile with assess-
ment, technical
skills; tension be-
tween written and
spoken

Media

most accessible form
of language open to
pupils – pervasive
direct and spin-off
effects – images,
attitudes, stereotyping
of cultures and
individuals

UNDERSTANDING
THINKING
FEELING
CREATING

Oracy

valuing the
spoken word
rather than sub-
ordinating it to
the written form
– oral heritage

Reading

need to teach
'reflexes' to be
critical rather
than allowing
fixed authority to
texts

Writing

links between
spoken and writ-
ten to get away
from ethnocentric
dominance

Drama

forum for risks in
role-playing invol-
ving empathy and
confrontation

Teacher Stance and Attitudes, Methods and Materials

Personal	*Emotional*	*Moral*	*Social*	*Political*
individual experience affecting attitude	'irrational' response rooted in conditioning	sense of 'right' 'wrong' defined by culture	influence of society – what expectations?	implicit and explicit motives behind

Parents, School, Community, Society

(Avon Multicultural Education Centre)

Chapter 6
Teacher Education and Professional Development

In this final chapter I turn to the issue of teacher education. After describing the current situation I provide a well tried model for short introductory in-service courses which aim to increase participants' understanding of key issues *and* their commitment to educational change. Finally I suggest ways in which individual teachers and educational managers can further their own professional development in multicultural education.

Minority Ethnic Group Teachers

Before considering the issue of teacher training (initial and in-service) we should note the relative lack of minority ethnic group teachers. A recent survey of eight local education authorities was undertaken for the CRE (Commission for Racial Equality) (Ranger, 1988). The overall picture which emerged from this was that ethnic minority teachers are few in number, that they are disproportionately on the lowest salary scales, and that they are concentrated in subjects where there is a shortage of teachers or where the 'special needs' of ethnic minority pupils are involved. They receive less encouragement and promotion and over half believed they had been discriminated against in this respect. There are no signs of a significant increase; in 1986 only 2.6 per cent of students in final year teacher training were of ethnic minority origin. Moreover, teachers from other countries (India and Pakistan) are often unable to obtain qualified teacher status in the UK. In some areas two year BEd degree courses, to cater for such teachers, have been developed. That the courses are shorter than other BEd programmes is at least some recognition of the teachers' previous training, qualifications and experience.

Obviously this situation is undesirable. Black and white pupils benefit from seeing black adults in a position of authority. Black pupils have a role model, and may sometimes find it helpful to have a teacher from their own ethnic background with whom to discuss their concerns.

Moreover, if we are to have the genuine, and not the tokenistic pluralism advocated in previous chapters then it is crucial that we have a much less homogenous teaching force than is currently the case. The CRE report makes several recommendations to this end: these include monitoring the number of ethnic minority teachers and student teachers and taking positive action to encourage applications from members of these groups; reviewing procedures for recruitment, promotion, re-scaling, in-service training and secondment applications, appointing selection panels, and allocating special responsibilities. Any disadvantages or direct or indirect discriminatory practices should be eliminated. Moreover, those responsible for nominating or appointing boards of Governors should make better use of the expertise and experience available in ethnic minority communities.

In May (1988) the DES (Department of Education and Science), issued a consultative document on qualified teacher status (QTS). The proposal for consideration is that people with certain (unspecified) minimal qualifications be employed as 'licensed teachers' and that, while in post, they receive additional training to become fully qualified teachers. Ethnic minority teachers are specifically mentioned in the document. Many people and interest groups have expressed various reservations about different parts of the proposals (for example they include the idea of dispensing with a probationary year for newly qualified staff). The CRE are concerned that the discretion permitted by this licence system for individual officers and governing bodies could prove fertile soil for yet more indirect institutional discrimination. However, if these proposals *do* come into effect, then (as with ERA) whatever retrogressive tendency they may have, it will be important to ensure that the new situation is used positively – to recruit and train more black teachers.

Initial and In-Service Teacher Training

The Swann Report underlines the need for two distinct forms of multicultural provision in teacher training: provision to give student teachers the particular knowledge and skills needed to teach in a multiracial school, and the preparation of all students for teaching in a multiracial society, in any school.

The report also emphasizes that such training cannot be done in a 'mechanistic' way, bolting on a multicultural bit. Rather, a multicultural awareness should permeate all aspects of training. Sociology, psychology and philosophy of education should take account of cultural diversity. Subject-specific courses should develop a multicultural dimension, for example by discussing the development of scientific and mathematical concepts in different cultures, and by broadening the range of literature, art and music.

There is much talk, generally, about the need for 'permeation' of a multicultural perspective – in teacher training, in pupils' learning experiences, and so on. The idea is that each aspect of the student teacher's learning contribute to their training to teach in a multicultural society. The permeation metaphor involves the idea that each part of training or education is impregnated with a pluralist dimension or perspective. Some curriculum areas are more readily 'permeated' than others, though more areas are currently ethnocentric, and could be pluralistically developed, than we tend to imagine.

In practice, however, little of this 'permeation' of initial training is taking place. For this reason, the Swann Report advocates, in the immediate future, reference to pluralist issues within the central and compulsory 'core' of the initial training received by all teachers. This would include basic information about immigration, the experiences of different minority groups and a study of racism at institutional and individual levels. Moreover, if a students teacher has deep-seated and openly racist views which do not appear to be open to change through training, this should be an important element in assessing whether he or she is suitable to enter the teaching profession.

The Swann Report also makes the point that the majority of teachers in schools today receive little or no multicultural provision in their initial training. Hence the importance of adequate provision at the 'in-service' stage. Unfortunately, as we know from a DES enquiry, '*In service Teacher Education in a Multicultural Society*' (Eggleston, 1980), such provision is fragmentary and incomplete. Some local education authorities provide no training in multicultural education, and in no LEA is it wholly adequate.

Swann advocates that any teacher entering a multiracial school for the first time should receive substantial induction training in the background knowledge needed to offer all pupils an appropriate education, free from stereotypes, and to recognize the opportunities offered in a multiracial setting.

Such induction would include: avoiding ethnocentrism within particular subjects, handling racism amongst pupils, relating to pupils from a wide range of backgrounds, meeting particular needs (for example in terms of language) and using, positively, the range of pupils' experiences within schools. Special short courses will be an important part of a wider staff development process. There is also urgent need to develop appropriate courses for teachers from 'all white' schools. This provision would include: informed awareness of the diversity of contemporary Britain, racism and how it can be challenged, and the idea of 'Education for All'.

These tasks for teacher education at both initial and in-service level entail the need for some retraining of the trainers themselves.

In this range of course provision, an important common element of most courses has been 'Racism Awareness Training' (RAT). What is RAT and why has it been criticized?

Racism Awareness Training

Racism awareness courses are explicitly focused on white racism in both its personal and institutional forms. The aim is to influence the attitudes and behaviour of the teachers who participate by increasing their understanding and awareness of how racism functions in education and in the wider society. The teaching approach is mainly based on experiential learning techniques: role play, audio-visual material, brainstorming, 'games', and simulations. Many of these experimental components, or similar ones, can be found in *'White Awareness': Handbook for Anti-racism Training* (Katz, 1978).

Good adult education has always relied on a diversity of teaching approaches, and, recognizing the adult status of learners and the way adults learn, relies more on discussion and shared analysis than on formal lectures. Certainly where it is hoped that participants will confront and modify their own prejudices, a preaching 'talk and chalk' approach would be particularly ineffective. The teaching approaches of RAT, therefore, make good sense both in relation to educating adults generally and in relation to the specific aims and objectives of these particular courses.

Nevertheless, RAT has been very widely criticized. The Right claim it is indoctrination imposed by the Left; others on the Left claim it amounts to a guilt inducing indulgence which changes nothing. some point out that most RAT courses are 'preaching to the converted', since only already 'aware' teachers elect to attend. Yet others claim that short courses with the 'unconverted' are at best ineffective, and at worse harden hostile attitudes.

The most important criticism is that to raise individual awareness of racism does not change structural racism in education. However, though education can never, by itself, effect social justice, it perhaps can play a small part in making some contribution in that direction. Individual racial prejudices and social discrimination interact and reinforce each other. For this reason anti-racism must fight on each level, and it is a mistake to eschew 'individual level' strategies. Individual prejudices perpetuate and legitimate institutional racism. (For a fuller discussion of this see: *Communicating Racism* by Teun A van Dijk, 1987.)

Of course RAT should, ideally, represent only one input among others in a teacher's professional development in anti-racist multicultural education, and some RAT courses are, no doubt, better than others. A good 'race and education' course would aim not just to allow teachers to confront their own racial prejudices but also to increase their understanding of the nature of prejudice and the nature of racism in our society and in our education system. In addition, it would provide teachers with an understanding of the nature of change and strategies for bringing about anti-racist changes in their school and in their own classroom practices. (Similarly, it would provide educational administrators with an understanding of strategies for bringing about such changes in their LEA and in their own administrative procedures). This presupposes the further aim that participants should develop an anti-racist commitment.

What follows is the outline of a model short course which incorporates all these dimensions. It is based on my experiences of running such courses in Birmingham and elsewhere, and, with the assistance of its multicultural support service, for the Avon LEA. Lack of resources hampered the follow up support ideally required, but, even so, the work was, in my view, worthwhile.

Model of an Introductory Short Course

The model should be modified to suit the particular participants, and the time and resources available. It can be added to for a longer programme. More complex learning experience could be incorporated, for more advanced learners. It provides an example of how a number of disparate but related educational aims and objectives can be catered for, within one coherent 'racism awareness' course.

The programme divides into three main blocks, focused respectively on:

(1) Understanding Racism

(2) The Nature of Change

(3)   Anti-Racism in Action.

Most RAT courses cover the material and stages found in block (1): Understanding Racism. The additional blocks (2) and (3) seek to provide participants with understanding and skills which will enable them to translate their increased awareness of racism into anti-racist educational change. Each block contains intellectual, affective and behavioural components and involves the development of interrelated knowledge, attitudes and skills.

It is important that the course ethos is one of professional competence and relevance. For example, for these courses in Avon, the tutors involved, from Avon's multicultural support service, ensured that participants arrived to a beautifully presented display of books, artifacts and posters on display stands round the main teaching area. It included good learning resources from the Multicultural Education Centre, the Schools Art Loan Service, the Library Service and the Hummingbird book shop. It also included a section contrasting positive images of black children and adult, with negative images. Handouts and worksheets were produced to a similar high standard.

The aims are set out (page 98) with corresponding session suggestions (page 99). Given that the aims involve individuals confronting and changing their own attitudes and making professional commitments, it is important that tutors are supportive. They should see their role as learning facilitators, and not as preachers or judges and should remember that any process of learning, of changing through learning, takes time.

Each of the aims can be broken down into a number of objectives, each of which will have at least one session devoted to its achievement. Thus the aim of 'increasing participants understanding of prejudice' incorporates the following objectives:

- to explore the concept of racial prejudice and its many forms;

- to understand the nature and functioning of stereotyping;

- to be aware of stereotyping in the media and in educational materials;

- to understand the relation between prejudice and discrimination;

- to explore the educational implication of the points listed above.

The sessions suggested are a sample of some key learning situations from each of the three blocks. Others can be added or substituted.

Once participants have been welcomed and have introduced themselves and talked about what they hope to get out of the course, a useful opening exercise is the analysis of 'prejudice' and 'racism'. Participants are provided with definition of these terms, and, in small groups, through discussion stimulated by these, work out their own definitions. Participants note down key points in their discussions, as well as the definitions they have agreed. As groups feed back these points and their definitions, key themes emerge. This kind of beginning is interesting. It allows participants to feel that they are working from a base of knowledge they already have, and are using their own definitions in discussions. Next a short formal input on different forms of racism can be followed by participants brainstorming actual examples.

Media studies is a good focus for understanding the racism of our society, and introduces concepts of bias, 'balance', image (positive and negative) and stereotyping. It also raises the issue of black employment too. How many producers are black? Use of black actors? For information, analysis and discussion two excellent BBC programmes can be used. (*The Black and White Media Show* I and II).

Continuing to use a variety of approaches, the focus next moves to racism in education. Sessions should deal with racial abuse, racism in the curriculum, in learning resources and school organization, and at LEA level. A black perspective, bringing out the anger, hurt and damage engendered by racism, is incorporated through speakers, videos and written extracts and articles which reproduce the experiences and reflections of black people. Several situations can be thought provoking, for instance an harassment situation is described, separately to small groups, with questions and comments encouraged. For some groups the harasser is white and the harassed is black. For other groups the racial identities are reversed. Did the white participants make the same judgements in each case? (White people tend to identify more readily with white victims and to take sterner judgements against black harassers.)

The final session of block (1) consists of the Katz – 'Designing A School' exercise. Participants brainstorm the different aspects which make up school life. (The facilitator records these.) They then divide into three groups. Group A designs an intentionally racist school; group B an unintentionally racist school and group C an anti-racist school. They share their descriptions at the end. These should be recorded on flip charts and kept for later use.

In my experience this session always works well. Participants enjoy it and learn a great deal. They see that racism or anti-racism make a difference to all aspects of school life. They understand more fully what is meant by unintentional racism, and recognize school (B) as their own.

Block (2) turns to the nature of institutional change. Formal input, discussion and handouts cover: the nature of institutional change; factors which hinder and which facilitate it; and strategies for securing complex and/or controversial changes. The National Development Centre have produced an analysis of key management tasks in education. (See page 77.)

Participants should work out the anti-racist, multicultural dimension of each of these tasks and then the strategies for developing this dimension. Having devoted time to change, in the final session of this block, participants turn once more to their recorded descriptions of racist (intentional and unintentional) and anti-racist schools. The task to be worked on is: given what they have learned about the nature of change and change strategies, how do we move from the features of schools A and B to the features of school C?

The final block is about setting realistic professional goals for participants' work after the course. Sessions provide an opportunity for participants to work out the potentialities for their own role (as teacher, head of department, headteacher or whatever). What powers to bring about educational change do they have? What difficulties may they have to face and what solutions might they find? What support will be available? In the penultimate session they should be provided with a sheet for recording short (one term), medium (one year) and long term (five year) goals. In pairs they discuss and finally individually record their own goals – which should be realistic and achievable. Where possible, course facilities should, ideally, be part of this contract by offering appropriate continuing support to help individuals achieve their goals. Obviously, this can only be the case where such ongoing contact and support is available. Similarly, and ideally, participants should be able to return for a follow up in-service day one year later. This provides a useful opportunity to discuss and analyse progress. What goals were or were not achieved and why? Participants will learn a great deal from the experiences of each other.

Finally, at the end of the (initial) course, participants should be asked to say, in turn, one positive idea they have gained. This ensures that the programme ends on a positive note, but also re-emphasizes some of the helpful practical ideas which emerged during the sessions.

The course organizers will find evaluation sheet invaluable for improving and developing the courses they offer.

Figure 6.1: Racism Awareness Course Aims – The Three Blocks

Block (1) – Understanding Racism

1. To increase understanding of the nature of endemic racial prejudices in our society and the education system.

2. To increase participants' awareness of their own racial prejudices and stereotyping.

3. To increase understanding of the nature of racial discrimination in our society and the education system.

4. To show how racism adversely affects people and provides opportunities for participants to experience a moral commitment to racial justice.

Block (2) – The Nature of Change

1. To increase understanding of the nature of change in institutions and of factors which facilitate and which hinder change.

2. To widen participants' knowledge of change strategies and to develop their skills as change agents.

3. To explore the management of change in the context of education.

4. To enable participants to see themselves as change agents with the power to effect change.

Block (3) – Anti-Racism: Goals and Contract

1. To enable participants to apply strategies for educational change in the context of anti-racist education.

2. To increase participants' awareness of how their own particular institutional role can contribute to anti-racism.

3. To provide the opportunity for participants to identify anti-racist changes which they could achieve.

4. To provide the opportunity for participants to enter a contract with themselves; i.e. to devise a realistic timetable of achievable anti-racist goals which they intend to achieve.

NB: Given four sessions per hard-working day, the minimum length of time for these 20 sessions is a *one-week* course.

Figure 6.2: Racism Awareness Course Suggested Sessions

Minimum no.
of sessions

Block (1) – Understanding Racism

1. Nature of Prejudice and Racism. Definition Sheets, etc.   2
2. Racism in the Media. Use of Black and White Media Videos, etc.   2
3. Racism in Education – including:-   6
   (a) Racial Abuse exercise (various situations described and discussed. How should I deal with each?)
   (b) Bias in Learning Materials – Analysis. Participants work out their own criteria for bias and then assess material randomly selected and brought from their school library and stockrooms.
   (c) Curriculum sessions. Input discussion.
   (d) ACER video – 'To School Together'.
       To show positive approach.
       Anti-racism as a natural part of typical primary school activities.
   (e) 'BAFA BAFA'. Simulation game.
       Generates useful insight into cultural racism.
   (f) The 'Designing Three Schools' exercise   1

Block (2) – The Nature of Change

1. The Nature of Change: Educational Change   2
2. Strategies for change.   1
3. The NDC Management Tasks (see p.77)   2
   Developing anti-racist dimension
   Managing its implementation
4. The 'Three Schools' Revisited (Moving from racist to anti-racist   1
      school)

Block (3) – Anti-Racism: Goals and Contract

1. Exploring ones role and its change potential.   1
2. Discussing and devising a *contract* with oneself.   1
3. A positive final session (and evaluation sheets).   1

Figure 6.3: Contract With Myself (Anti-Racist Multicultural Education)

Short-term Goals (one term)
  1.
  2.
  3.

Medium-term Goals (one year)
  1.
  2.
  3.

Long-term Goals (five years)
  1.
  2.
  3.

NB: The contract to be set out on A4 paper.

Professional Development

Any teacher who wishes to find out more about multicultural education will think about attending a local, regional or national introductory short course. As interest grows, with a conviction of the importance of this aspect of education, s/he is likely to attend national conferences and more specialized short courses and perhaps to undertake longer term studies through a part-time, or (if secondment is available) full-time enrolment at a local University or Polytechnic or perhaps with the Open University.

In addition to such courses and conferences, professional development can and should take other forms. Each of us has some responsibility for our own continuing education as teachers and should attempt to keep well informed about new reports (such as Swann) and those from bodies such as the CRE. Reading for development in anti-racist multicultural education should begin with a study of racism in our society and in the education system. There are several seminal books and many useful books and videos. Note particularly the reading recommended in the resource section (pages 104–108).

Teachers in multiracial schools have the advantage of dialogue with minority ethnic group parents who should be part of the life of the school. Teachers in white schools can network with others who share their interest – making contact with multicultural advisers, support services, relevant societies, good inner city schools, and so on.

Perhaps the most effective form of professional development is that which occurs through actually working with others on an anti-racist project of some kind. Some schools are able to benefit from school based INSET – through an in-service day, or even through a support service team of teachers working in and with the school. If all the staff cannot (or will not) be involved it may be possible to link with a smaller group of interested colleagues within the school, for a specific task. For example, to form a working party to look at school learning resources. In working out, together, what a balanced learning stock should be like, much learning will take place. Inevitably, you are led to consider issues about bias, ethnocentricity and stereotyping, to work out criteria for book selection and to discuss the thorny questions about which books, if any, should be removed from your shelves. This kind of process, which occurs when a group of people seek to make anti-racism progress, is invaluable. it provides a rich learning experience for those involved and simultaneously brings about, however modest, some worthwhile change in their particular school.

For a white teacher it is important to be open to a black perspective on these issues. By 'black perspective' I mean the point of view of those who most experience (on a daily basis) the injustice of racial abuse and discrimination – in subtle, overt, unintentional and deliberate forms. Thus one will be particularly interested in books and talks on racism by black authors, watch (the few) documentaries by black writers and producers, and listen to black pupils, parents and educationalists.

It must be admitted that all of the foregoing is time consuming and energy demanding. Moreover, there are many other crucial aspects of education which demand more learning or updating and make further inroads in a busy teacher's time. To answer this valid point, I would reiterate the importance of multicultural education in its own right, and would add that the issues it raises are wide ranging, overlap and interrelate with other important issues and often connect with debates at the heart of the educational task. For example, dialect issues are relevant to white working class as well as black children; discrimination issues widen our awareness in connection with other forms of oppression – sexism, heterosexism, etc. and any thinking about curriculum development will inevitably make us think hard about our fundamental aims and objectives. As a black advisory colleague once suggested to me, black people act as a kind of 'barium meal' in the system – throwing into relief and showing up (in both senses of this phrase) the social structures by which our society perpetuates its divisions of privilege and disadvantage.

Glossary

Background Terms for Chapter One

monocultural   pertains to one cultural tradition, e.g. only
                    Christianity in RE (Religious Education).

ethnocentric   a perspective so restricted to one cultural tradition as
                    to distort understanding, e.g. seeing Divali as 'The
                    Hindu Christmas'.

cultural pluralism an ideology of equality of standing between
                    different cultural groups.

racism   sometimes explained by reference to the slogan
                    Prejudice + Power = Racism. In other words,
                    negative discrimination by those individuals or
                    groups with power against the relatively
                    powerless, where the discrimination is based on
                    race (e.g. skin colour) or ethnicity.

anti-racism   simply – against racism. Anti-racist education
                    counters racism in and through education.

The following terms receive fuller analysis in Chapter 2, Section 1:

Race, immigrants, black, minority ethnic group, special needs, racial
prejudice, racial discrimination, institutional racism, pluralism.

Common Abbreviations

CRE   Commission for Racial Equality. Developed from
                 the Community Relations Commission to support
                 the Race Relations Act of 1976.

E2L   English as a second language. An abbreviation
                 commonly used in the context of English teaching/
                 learning and pupils whose first language is other
                 than English.

Section 11   Section 11 refers to the part of the 1966
                 Education Act (GB. DES, 1966) which provides for
                 the Home Office to make grants to local authorities
                 towards salary costs for people working to meet the
                 'special or additional need of people of New
                 Commonwealth origin'.

LEA   Local Education Authority.

Bibliography and Learning Resources

The suggestions for further reading have been divided into theoretical and more practical sections covering racism and race and education. In addition there is a book section on the curriculum. Each section includes a small number of relatively recent key texts. There are also suggestions about learning resources and a list of bibliographies from which much more comprehensive 'resource' information can be obtained. Teachers should select reading from each book section. At the very minimum read the Runnymede Trust (concise) summaries of the Swann and Eggleston Reports and the Trust's *Different Worlds*. It is also useful to have one's own copy of one of the resource bibliographies (for example G. Klein's *Resources for Multicultural Education: An Introduction*).

Further Reading: Theoretical

Racism

BARKER, M. (1980). *The New Racism*. Junction Books.
FRYER, P. (1984). *Staying Power: History of Black People in Britain*. London: Pluto Press.
OPEN UNIVERSITY (1983). *Racism in the Community and Workplace*. Milton Keynes: OU Press.
POLICY STUDIES INSTITUTE (1985). *Racial Discrimination Seventeen Years After the Act*. London: PSI Report 646.
REX, J. and TOMLINSON, S. (1979). *Colonial Immigrants in a British City*. Routledge and Kegan Paul.
SCARMAN REPORT (1981). *The Brixton Disorders 10–12 April 1981*. West Drayton: Penguin.
SIVANANDAN, A. (1982). *A Different Hunger: Writings on Black Resistance*. London:Pluto Press.

TEUN A VAN DIJK (1987). *Communicating Racism, Ethnic Prejudice in Thought and Talk*. Beverly Hills, CA: Sage Publications Inc.

Race and Education

CARRINGTON, B. and SHORT, G. (1989). *'Race' and the Primary School: Theory into Practice*. Windsor: NFER-NELSON.
EDWARDS, V.K. (1979). *The West Indian Issue in British Schools*. London: Routledge and Kegan Paul.
EGGLESTON REPORT (1987). *Education for Some. (See References.)*
HAYDON, G. (ed.) (1987). *Education for a Pluralist Society. Philosophical perspectives on the Swann Report*. London: Institute of Education.
JAMES, A. and JEFFCOATE, R. (eds) (1981). *The School in the Multicultural Society*. London: Harper and Row.
JOURNAL OF MORAL EDUCATION (1986). *Race, Culture and Education* (Special Issue), Vol 15 No 1. Windsor: NFER-NELSON.
MILNER, D. (1983). *Children and Race: Ten Years On. London: Ward Lock*.
Ethnic Minorities and Education, Course E354 Units 13–14 Block 4. Milton Keynes: Open University.
STONE, M. (1981). *The Education of the Black Child in Britain: The Myth of Multicultural Education*. London: Fontana.
SWANN REPORT (1985). *Education for All*. (See References.)
TIERNEY, I. (ed.) (1982). *Race, Migration and Schooling*. New York: Holt, Rinehart and Winston.
VERMA, G.K. and BAGLEY, C. (eds) (1979). *Race, Education and Identity*. London and Basingstoke: Macmillan.
WILLEY, R. (1984). *Race, Equality and School*. London: Methuen.

NB: The Runnymede Trust has summarized the Swann Report and also the Eggleston Report. Each available from the Runnymede Trust, 37A Grays Inn Road, London, WC1 8PP, 40p plus postage and packing.

Further Reading: More Practical

Racism

ALTARF (ALL LONDON TEACHERS AGAINST RACISM AND FACISM) from Unit 216, Panther House, 38 Mount Pleasant, London WC1X OAP.

BERGER, J. (1975). *A Seventh Man ... Migrant Workers in Europe.* West Drayton: Penguin Books.

ILEA (INNER LONDON EDUCATION AUTHORITY) (1979) *Our Lives. Young people's autobiographies.* English Centre.

INSTITUTE OF RACE RELATIONS. *Roots of Racism* (1982), *Patterns of Racism* (1982). *How Racism Came to Britain* (1984) and *The Fight Against Racism* (1986).

KATZ, J. (1978). *White Awareness: Handbook for Anti-Racism Training*, University of Oklahoma Press.

PRESCOD-ROBERTS, M. and STEELE, N. (1980). *Black Women: bringing it all back home.* Falling Wall Press.

RUNNYMEDE TRUST (1983). *Different Worlds: Racism and Discrimination in Britain.* Runnymede Trust.

STINTON, I. (ed.) (1981). *Racism and Sexism in Children's Books*, Writers and Readers. (distributor: Airlift Book Co., London.)

Race and Education

AFFOR (1982). *Talking Chalk, Black pupils, parents and teachers speak about education.* AFFOR.

ARORA, R. and DUNCAN, C. (eds) (1986). *Multicultural Education. Towards Good Practice.* London: Routledge and Kegan Paul.

BULMERSHE COLLEGE OF HIGHER EDUCATION (1983). *A Fair Hearing for All: Relationship between Teaching and Racial Equality.*

GAINE, C. (1987). *No Problem Here. A practical approach to education and 'race' in white schools.* London: Hutchinson.

ILEA. *Education in a Multi-Ethnic Society – a aide-memoire for the Inspectorate..* ILEA learning material service, Station Road, London, N1 1SB.

KLEIN, G. (1985). *Reading into Racism: Bias in Children's Literature and Learning Material.* London: Routledge and Kegan Paul.

MINORITY RIGHTS GROUP (1985 edn). *Teaching About Prejudice.* London MRG.

NIXON, J. (1985). *A Teacher's Guide to Multicultural Education*. Oxford: Basil Blackwell.

STENHOUSE, L. *et al.* (1982). *Teaching About Race Relations. Problems and Effects*. London: Routledge and Kegan Paul.

STRAKER-WELD, M. (ed.) (1984). *Education for a Multicultural Society. Case Studies in ILEA Schools*, Bell and Hyman. (London: Unwin Hyman).

TWITCHEN, J. and DEMUTH, C. (1981). *Multicultural Education*, BBC.

WILLEY, R. (1982). *Teaching in Multicultural Britain*, Schools Council.

Curriculum

ARORA, R. and DUNCAN, C. (eds) (1986). *Multicultural Education. Towards Good Practice*. London: Routledge and Kegan Paul. Contains curriculum chapters on several school 'subjects'.

CRAFT, A. and BARDELL, G. (eds) (1984) *Curriculum opportunities in a Multicultural Society*. London: Harper Education. Focuses on most secondary school 'subjects'.

CRAFT, A. and KLEIN, G. (1986). *Agenda for Multicultural Teaching*. Harlow: Longman. Part Two is on *Curriculum matters* and covers most curriculum areas – with suggested books and resources.

KLEIN, G. (1982). *Resources for Multicultural education: an introduction*. Harlow: Longman. Section (3) *Concerning Curriculum* provides reading lists in Language; World Studies, General Studies and Social Studies; Religious Studies; Arts; Maths and Science; Home Economics and Discussing Race Relations in the Classroom.

LYNCH, J. (ed) (1981) *Teaching in the Multicultural School*. London: Ward Lock.

SCHOOL COUNCIL (SCP 1981). *Education for a Multicultural Society: Curriculum and Context 5–13*.

Bibliographies

CRAFT, A and KLEIN, G. (1986). *Agenda for Multicultural Teaching*. Harlow: Longman.

ELKIN, J. (1980). *Multiracial books for the classroom*. From Central Children's Library, Birmingham B3 3HQ.

EVANS, R. *Education in a Multicultural Society: a selected bibliography*. From Kiln Cottage, Culham, nr Abingdon, Oxon.

KLEIN, G. (1982). *Resources for Multicultural Education: An Introduction*. Harlow: Longman. This itself contains a list of bibliographies covering specific aspects of multicultural education, e.g. on South Asia and on China from the School of Oriental and African Studies. It also contains a list of *Criteria for Selecting Classroom Materials*. There are other published selection criteria including:

ACER (AFRO-CARIBBEAN EDUCATION RESOURCE) in their *Images and Reflections*. ACER 1982.

Learning Resources

Organizations

Commission for Racial Equality (CRE), Elliot House, 10/12 Allington Street, London SW1. Tel 01–828–7022.

Commonwealth Institute, Kensington High Street, London W8. Tel 01–602–3252. In addition to books, audio-visual aids and publications to borrow and buy, the Commonwealth Institute has display galleries on each Commonwealth County. These can be visited by school groups.

Minority Arts Advisory Service (MAAS), Beauchamp Lodge, 2 Warwick Crescent, London W2. Tel 01–286–1854. Publishes annual register of performers and teachers of the performing arts.

Runnymede Trust, 37a Grays Inn Road, London WC1. Tel. 01–405–7703. Lists of their publications are available + monthly Runnymede Trust bulletin.

Oxfam Education Department, 274 Banbury Road, Oxford, OX2 7D2 (tel. 0865–56777): has Development Education Centres in several areas and materials for teachers. (Write for catalogue.)

School of Oriental and African Studies (SOAS), University of London, Malet Street, London WC1. Tel. 01– 637–2388. Library, papers, bibliographies and resource centre.

SHAP (Working party on world religions.) Advice service for teachers: City of Liverpool College of Higher Education, Liverpool Road, Prescot, Merseyside. (Enclose SAE).

Classroom Material

ACER (The Afro-Caribbean Education Resource Centre), Wyvil
School, Wyvil Road, London, SW8 2TJ. Tel. 01–627–2662. Materi-
als for teachers and packs for pupils. Primary age range; project
work.
Anthologies – Prose and verse anthologies are available, for example
HALLWORTH, G. (1984). *Mouth Open, Story Jump Out*, Methuen.
ASH, A. (ed.) (1980). *Short Stories from India, Pakistan and Ban-
gladesh*,
BERRY, J. (1982). *Bluefoot Traveller*, Harrap. *H~w Strong The Roots:
Poems of Exile*, (1980) Evans and *Caribbean Anthology*, ILEA
Learning Materials Service. 1980 (with cassette).
'Ba Fa Ba Fa'. In HICKS, D. (1981) *Minorities*. pp. 82–5. A cross-
cultural simulation game. London and Oxford: Heinemann.
Bilingual/Community Languages. HEOSHIP, P. (1980–84). *Terraced
House Readers*, London: Methuen. These early reading books have
paste-on translations in several languages including Bengali, Pan-
jabi, Urdu and Turkish. INGHAM, J. (ed.). *Dual-Languagen story
books*, Luzac Publishers, 46 Great Russell Street, London, WC1B
3PE (traditional tales).
Development Education – Teaching Development Issues (1986). Devel-
opment Education Project.
FISHER, F. and HICKS, D. (1985). *World Studies 8–13*, Oliver and Boyd,
Much resource information and programmes of study.
ILEA – Catalogue of Primary Resources – from Centre for Learning
Resources, 225 Kennington Lane, London SE11 5QZ
ILEA English Centre. *The English Curriculum: Race: Materials for
Discussion*, English Centre (ILEA), Sutherland Street, London, SW1.
Journals. There are several useful journals. Investigate in multicultural
centres. For much current practical classroom based information see
Multicultural Teaching (3 issues per year), 30 Wenger Crescent,
Trentham, Stoke on Trent ST4 8LE.
Migration – Teaching about Migration (leaflet and catalogue), Centre
for World Development Education, Regent's College, Inner Circle,
Regent's Park, London, NW1 4NS.
Photopack. On Bangaldesh, India, Jamaica and Botswana from Oxfam
(address – see Organizations).
12 Posters on Colonialism – Whose World Is the World? Poster Film
Collective. BCM PFC London WC1N 3XX.

RICHARDSON, R. (1978). Four classroom books. *Fighting Freedom; World Conflict, Caring for the Planet; Progress and Poverty*. Walton-on-Thames: Nelson.
SHAP Calendar of Religious Festivals – available annually from CRE (Commission for Racial Equality).

Audio Visual Resources

Videos

ACER videos. *To School Together*. Contains useful material for teachers about permeating primary work with an anti-racist multicultural perspective. Wyvil School, Wyvil Road, London SW8 2TJ.
Africa. A series on the history of black Africa, available from the Commonwealth Institute, Kensington High Street, London W8.
The Black and White Media Show, two excellent BBC programmes in their Continuing Education series. Suitable for older pupils and adults.
The Eye of the Storm , film about a teacher generating prejudice in a primary school classroom on the basis of eye colour. Available from Concord Films, 201 Felixstowe Rd, Ipswich, Suffolk.
It Ain't Half Racist Mum, made in the BBC Open Door series. Available from Concord Films, 201 Felixstowe Rd, Ipswich, Suffolk. Suitable for older secondary pupils.
Our People. One on immigration myths, another on discrimination, and one on the colonial background. For availability contact Thames Schools' Television Publications Office, 149 Tottenham Court Road, W1P 9LL.
Racism, the 4th 'R', made by school pupils. ALTARF, c/o Lambeth Teachers' Centre, Santley St, London, SW4.
Teaching About Prejudice, BBC. Available from Concord Films, 201 Felixstowe Rd, Ipswich, Suffolk.

Filmstrips/tapeslides

The Enemy Within, Catholic Commission for Racial Justice, 1981. Available from the Bristol Council of Churches, 2 Eaton Gate, London SW1. Suitable for older pupils and adults.

Racism and Immigration, Mary Glasgow Publications, 140 Kensington Church St, London W8 4BN. With accompanying teacher's booklets.
Recognizing Racism. Made by David Ruddell. Available from Birmingham Minority Support Services.

Local Resources

Bookshops. There are specialist bookshops in many towns across Britain and some good library provision.
Voluntary Organizations. Relevant local organizations have resources of various kinds, e.g. visiting speakers, libraries, publications, classroom materials. Contact your Community Relations Council for information about local groups.
LEA (Local Education Authority) Support Services. Many LEAs have Multicultural Centres, library services, art loan services, multicultural advisers, etc.

References

ALEXANDER, Z. and DEWJEE, A.. (eds) (1984). *Wonderful Adventures of Mary Secole in Many Lands*. Falling Wall Press.

ALLPORT, W.H. (1958) *Prejudice*. New York: Doubleday.

BALL, W. (1987). 'Local Education Authority Policy Making on Equal Opportunities: Corporate Provision, Co-option and Consultation'. *Policy and Politics*. 15(2) 101–110.

BEN-TOVIN, G. *et al.* (1986). *The Local Politics of Race*. London and Basingstoke: Macmillan.

BERG, L. (1976). *Folk tales for reading and telling*. London: Pan Books.

BULLOCK REPORT. GREAT BRITAIN. DEPARTMENT OF EDUCATION AND SCIENCE. (1975). *A Language for Life*. London: HMSO.

EGGLESTON, J. (1988). 'Windows of Opportunity' in *Multicultural Teaching*. Vol. 6 No. 3, Stoke-on-Trent: Trentham Books.

EGGELSTON REPORT. GREAT BRITAIN. DEPARTMENT OF EDUCATION AND SCIENCE. (1987). *Education for Some – Vocational and Educational Experience of Young People from Ethnic Minority groups*. London: HMSO.

EGGLESTON, S.J. *et al.* (1980). *In Service Teacher Education in Multi-racial Society*. Keele: University of Keele.

FLEW, A. (1984). *Education, Race and Revolution*, London Centre for Policy Studies.

FORUM. 1988. Editorial.

FOSTER, E. 'Careers'. In DUNCAN, C. (1988). *Pastoral Care*. Oxford: Basil Blackwell.

GAINE, C. (1987). *No Problem Here*: A practical approach to education and "race" in white schools. London: Hutchinson.

GRINTER, R. (1985). In: *Multicultural Teaching*. Vol. 3 No. 2.

HAYDON, G. (ed.), (1987). *Education for a Pluralist Society*. London: Trentham Books Institute of Education.

KATZ, J. (1978). *White Awareness: A Handbook for Anti-racism Training*, Norman, Oklahoma: University of Oklahoma Press.

KLEIN, G. (1982). *Resources for Multicultural Education: an Introduction*. Harlow: Longman.

LEICESTER, M. (1986). In: *Multicultural Teaching*. Vol. 4 No. 2.

LOCAL GOVERNMENT ACT, GREAT BRITAIN, HOME OFFICE (1966).

LUKES, S. (1974). 'Relativism: Cognitive and Moral'. In: *Proceedings of the Aristotelian Society*. Supp. Vol. XL VIII.

MILNER, D. (1983). *Children and Race Ten Years On*. London: Ward Lock.

NATIONALITY ACT, GREAT BRITAIN, HOME OFFICE (1983).

NIXON, J. (1985). *Multicultural Education*. Oxford: Basil Blackwell.

PETERS, R.S. (1966). *Ethnics and Education*. Allen and Unwin. (London: Unwin Hyman).

PHILLIPS-BELL, M. *et al.* (1983). *Issues and Resources*, AFFOR.

RAMPTON REPORT. GREAT BRITAIN. DEPARTMENT OF EDUCATION AND SCIENCE, (1981). *West Indian Children In Our Schools*. London: HMSO.

RANGER, C. (1988). *Ethnic Minority School Teachers, A survey in eight LEAs*. London: CRE.

SCARMAN REPORT. GREAT BRITAIN. DEPARTMENT OF EDUCATION AND SCIENCE, (1982). *Inquiry into the Brixton disorders*. London: HMSO.

SCHOOLS COUNCIL. (1981). *Education for a Multicultural Society*, Schools Council.

SEALEY, A. (1983). 'Primary School Projects: a multicultural approach'. In: *Issues and Resources*, AFFOR.

STONE, M. (1981). *The Education of the Black Child in Britain: The Myth of Multicultural Education*. London: Fontana.

STRAKER-WELD, M. (ed.) (1984). 'Education for a multicultural Society: Case Studies in ILEA Schools'. London: Unwin Hyman.

Summary of The Swann Report, (1985). Runnymede Trust.

SWANN REPORT. GREAT BRITAIN. DEPARTMENT OF EDUCTION AND SCIENCE, (March, 1985). *Education For All*. London: HMSO.

VAN DIJK, T.A. (1987). *Communicating Racism. Ethnic Prejudice in Thought and Talk*. London: SAGE Publications.

WATTS, and LAW. In: FOSTER, E. (Article mentioned above).

WHITAKER, P. In: LANG, P. (ed.) (1988). *Personal and Social Education*. Oxford: Basil Blackwell.

WHITE, J. In: *Education for a Pluralist Society*. London: Institute of Education.

WINCH, P. (1958). 'Understanding A Primitive Society'. In: *The Idea of a Social Science and its Relation to Reality*. London: Routledge and Kegan Paul.